Contents

1a

SKILL

Opening a New Document and using Save As

Opening a new document

1 Click **File**.

2 Click **New**.

3 Click the **General** tab.

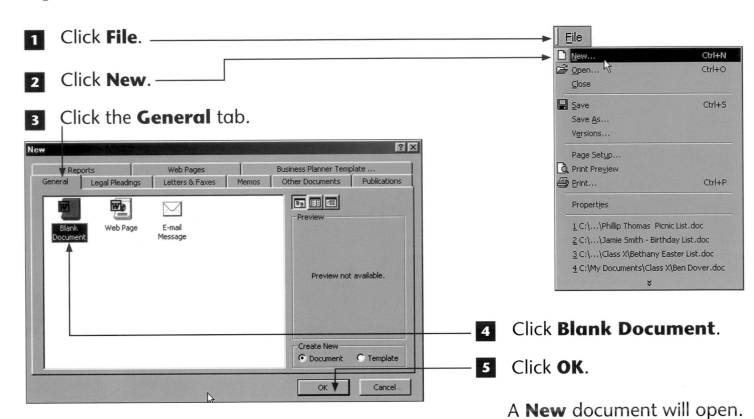

4 Click **Blank Document**.

5 Click **OK**.

A **New** document will open.

Saving a new document

6 Click **File**.

7 Click **Save As**.

8 Type your name.

9 Click **Save**.

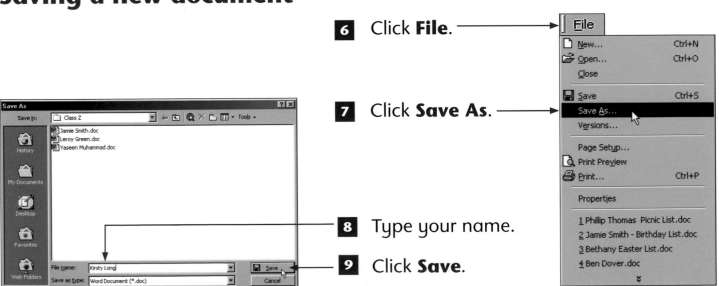

WordWorks

Write a Shopping List

SKILL: Opening a New Document and using Save As

APPLICATION

1 Open a **New** document. (See 1a)

2 Type your name and what your shopping list is for. Here are some examples:

> Michael Taylor. Christmas List

> Emily. Birthday List

3 Press **Enter**.

4 Now type your list. Press **Enter** after each item.

5 **Save** your work, call it by your name and the name of your shopping list. (See 1a)

6 Do this task again but use the icons at the top of the screen. (Go back to **1**)

New

Save

Opening an existing document

1 Click **File**. ————————————————————————

2 Click **Open**. ————————————————————————

3 Click the File that you want to open.
It will highlight in blue.

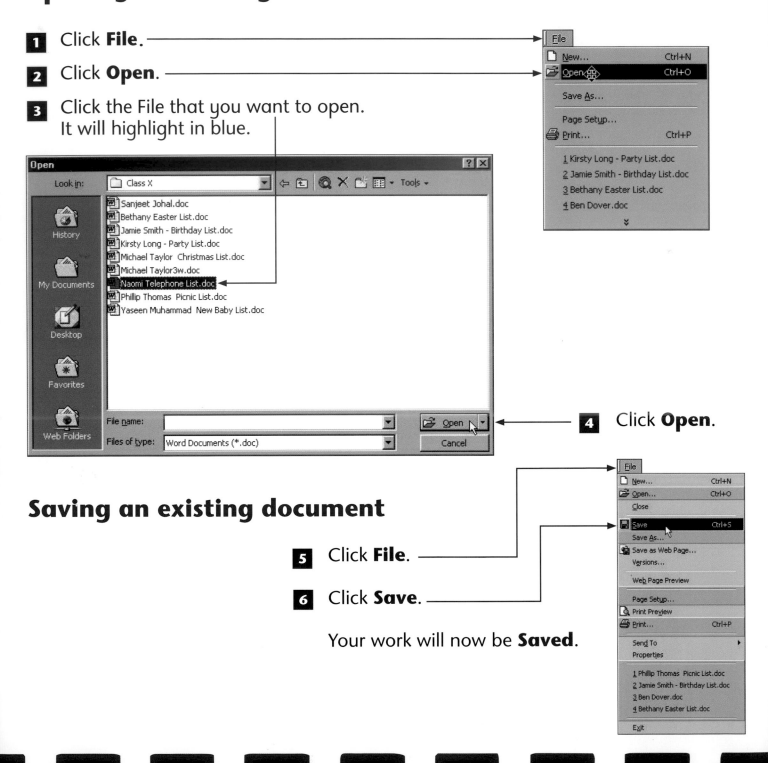

4 Click **Open**.

Saving an existing document

5 Click **File**. ————————

6 Click **Save**. ————————

Your work will now be **Saved**.

WordWorks

Add Items to your List

SKILL: Opening an Existing Document and using Save

1 **Open** your shopping list File. (See 2a)

2 Add two more items to your list.

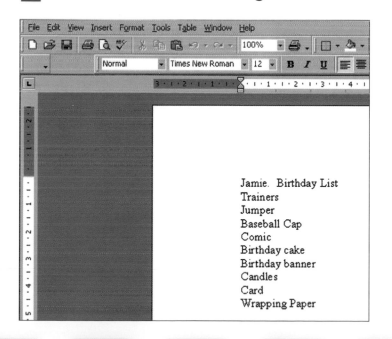

3 **Save** your work. (See 2a)

4 Do this task again but use the icons at the top of the screen. (Go back to **1**)

Open

Save

WordWorks 7

3a SKILL

1 To **Save** any document to disk, click **File**. ──────────▶

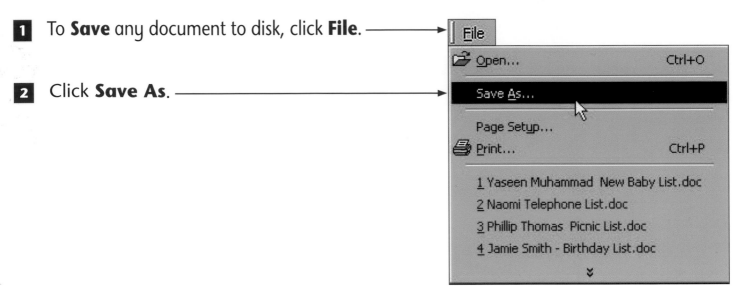

File

🗁 Open...	Ctrl+O
Save As...	
Page Setup...	
🖨 Print...	Ctrl+P

1 Yaseen Muhammad New Baby List.doc
2 Naomi Telephone List.doc
3 Phillip Thomas Picnic List.doc
4 Jamie Smith - Birthday List.doc
⌄

2 Click **Save As**. ─────────────────────────────▶

3 Click the arrow.

A list of locations will appear.

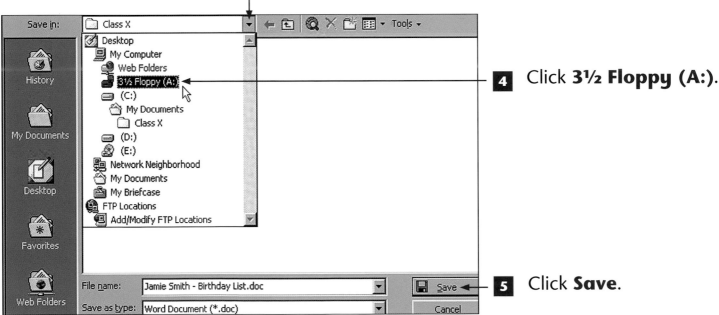

Save in:	Class X

Desktop
My Computer
Web Folders
3½ Floppy (A:)
(C:)
My Documents
Class X
(D:)
(E:)
Network Neighborhood
My Documents
My Briefcase
FTP Locations
Add/Modify FTP Locations

History
My Documents
Desktop
Favorites
Web Folders

4 Click **3½ Floppy (A:)**.

File name:	Jamie Smith - Birthday List.doc	💾 Save
Save as type:	Word Document (*.doc)	Cancel

5 Click **Save**.

Your work will now be **Saved** on disk.

1 **Open** your shopping list File. (See 2a)

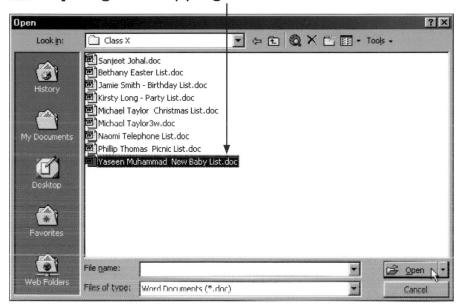

2 Add three shops where you can buy the items on your list.

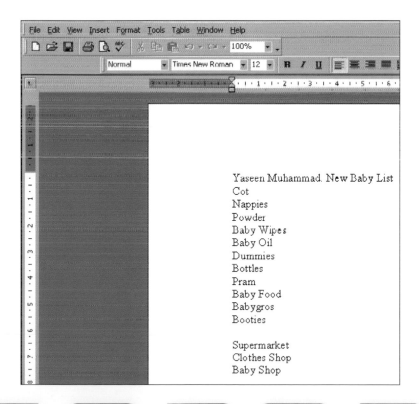

3 **Save** to disk. (See 3a)

4a

SKILL

Closing a File

Always **Save** before closing. (See 2a)

1 Click **File**. ────────────────────────

2 Click **Close**. ───────────────────────

*What if I forget to **Save**?*

● A box will appear asking if you want to **Save** the changes.

● Click **Yes**.

File menu:
- New... Ctrl+N
- Open... Ctrl+O
- Close
- Save Ctrl+S
- Save As...
- Versions...
- Page Setup...
- Print Preview
- Print... Ctrl+P
- Properties
- 1 Phillip Thomas Picnic List.doc
- 2 Michael Taylor3w.doc
- 3 Kirsty Long - Party List.doc
- 4 Jamie Smith - Birthday List.doc

● The File will then be **Saved** and **Closed**.

Exiting Word

3 You can **Exit** *Word* in two ways:

● Click the cross in the top right-hand corner of your screen.

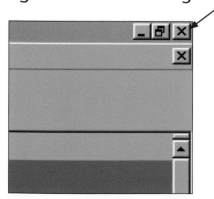

OR

● Click **File**. ──

● Click **Exit**. ──

File menu:
- New... Ctrl+N
- Open... Ctrl+O
- Close
- Save Ctrl+S
- Save As...
- Save as Web Page...
- Versions...
- Web Page Preview
- Page Setup...
- Print Preview
- Print... Ctrl+P
- Send To ▶
- Properties
- 1 Phillip Thomas Picnic List.doc
- 2 Michael Taylor3w.doc
- 3 Kirsty Long - Party List.doc
- 4 Jamie Smith - Birthday List.doc
- Exit

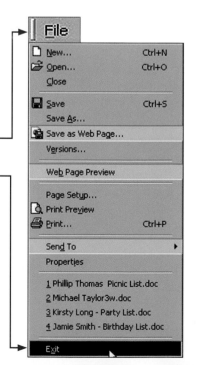

Describe Me

SKILL: Closing a File and Exiting Word

APPLICATION

1 Open a **New** document. (See 1a)

2 Type your full name.

3 Press **Enter**.

4 List three features that describe how you look.

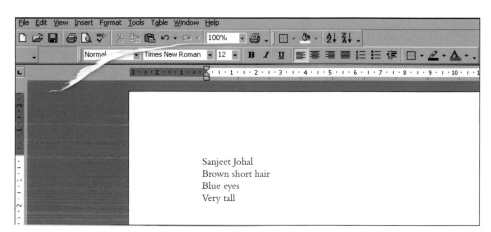

Sanjeet Johal
Brown short hair
Blue eyes
Very tall

5 **Save** your work. (See 1a)

6 **Close** your work. (See 4a)

7 **Exit** *Word*.

1 Open a **New** document. (See 1a)

2 Click the arrow next to the **Font** name.

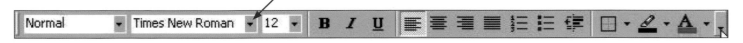

A list of all the different **Fonts** will appear underneath.

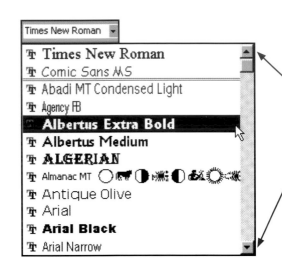

3 Click the arrows to see the different **Font** styles.

4 Click the one you want.

When you type, the text will appear in the **Font** that you chose.

*What if I forgot to change the **Font** before I started typing?*

● **Highlight** your text by dragging the I over it, holding down the left mouse button.

● Now you can change the **Font**. (Go back to **2**)

● Click anywhere on the screen.

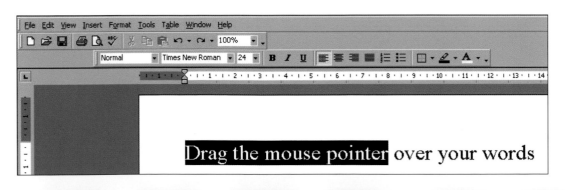

Drag the mouse pointer over your words

People in My Class

SKILL: Changing Font

1 Open a **New** document.

2 Select a **Font** to use. (See 5a)

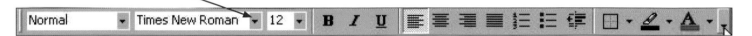

3 Type your name.

4 Press **Enter**. Now type your class name or number.

5 **Highlight** your class name by dragging the I over it, holding down the left button and change the **Font**.

6 Pick a different **Font** from the one that you chose for your name.

7 Type a list of the boys and girls in your class.

8 Choose one **Font** for the girls and a different one for the boys.

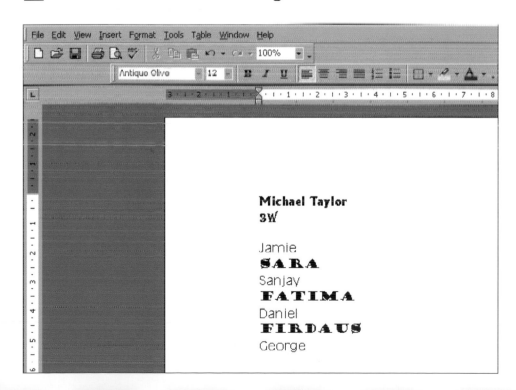

9 **Save** your work. (See 1a)

1 Open a **New** document.

2 Click the arrow next to the **Font Size** number.

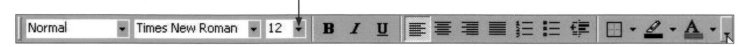

A list of **Font Sizes** will appear.

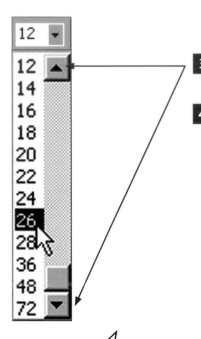

3 Click the arrows to see the **Font Sizes**.

4 Click the **Font Size** you want.

When you type, your text will appear in the **Font Size** that you chose.

What if I forgot to change the **Font Size** *before I started typing?*

• **Highlight** your text by dragging the I over it, holding down the left mouse button.

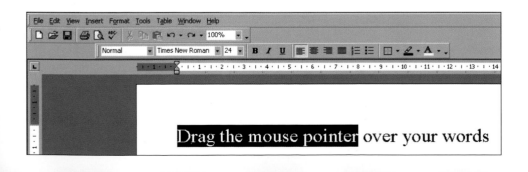

• Now you can change the **Font Size**. (Go back to **2**)

• Click anywhere on the screen.

From Small to Gigantic

1 Type the following words and change the **Font Size** of the words to match the meaning. (See 6a)

Small	Tiny
Large	Massive
Miniature	Gigantic

2 Type three other words that you could use to describe size and change their **Font Size** to match the meaning.

3 **Save** your work.

4 **Close** your File and **Exit** Word. (See 4a)

Changing Font Colour

Changing the colour of text

1 Open a **New** document.

2 Click the arrow next to the **Font Color** (**Colour**) icon.

The different **Font Colours** will appear.

3 Click the **Font Color** (**Colour**) of your choice.

When you type, your text will appear in that **Font Colour**.

*What if I forgot to change the **Font Colour** before I started typing?*

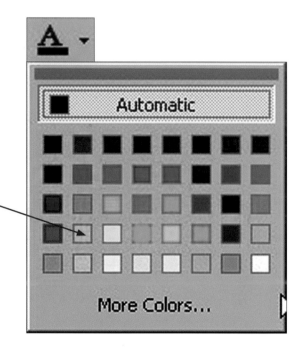

Automatic

More Colors...

● **Highlight** your text by dragging the I over it, holding down the left mouse button.

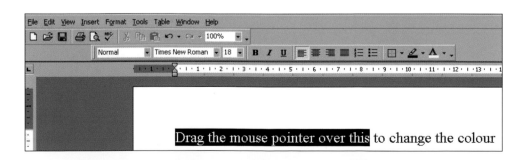

Drag the mouse pointer over this to change the colour

● Now you can change the **Font Colour**. (Go back to **2**)

● Click anywhere on the screen.

Find a Matching Font Colour

SKILL: Changing Font Colour

1 Open a **New** document.

2 Type each of the following words using the **Font Colour** that matches it. (See 7a)

The first one is done for you.

Elephant

Ruby

Daffodil

Sea

Sand

Grass

3 Add five words of your own.

4 Now type your full name using a different **Font Colour** for each of the letters.

5 **Save** your work. (See 2a)

8a

SKILL

Printing your work

To **Print** any document:

1 Click **File**.

2 Click **Print**.

> *The name of your printer will appear here.*

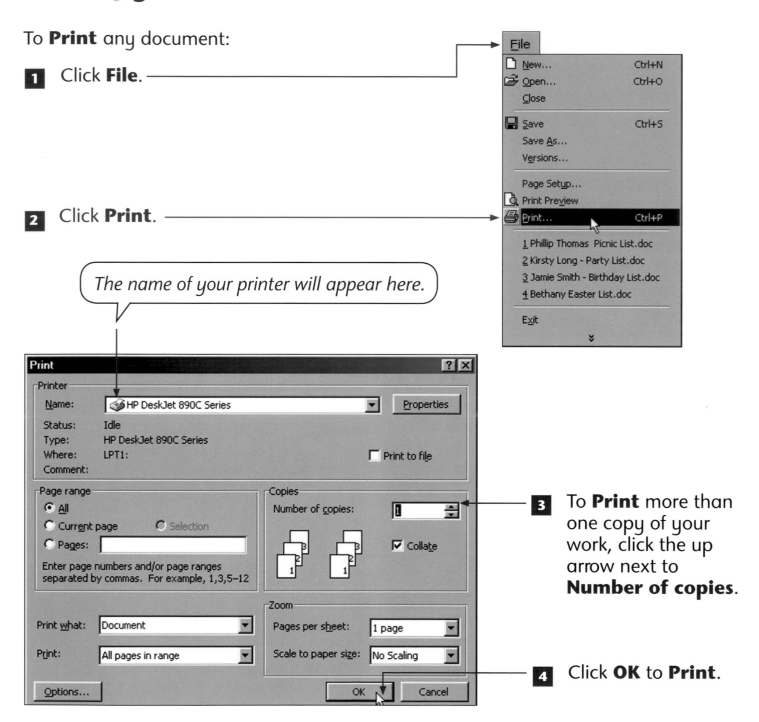

3 To **Print** more than one copy of your work, click the up arrow next to **Number of copies**.

4 Click **OK** to **Print**.

My Birthday List

SKILL: Printing

1 Open a **New** document.

2 Type your name.

3 Press **Enter**.

4 Now type a list of things that you would like for your birthday. Press **Enter** after each item.

5 **Save** your work.

6 **Print** two copies of your birthday list.

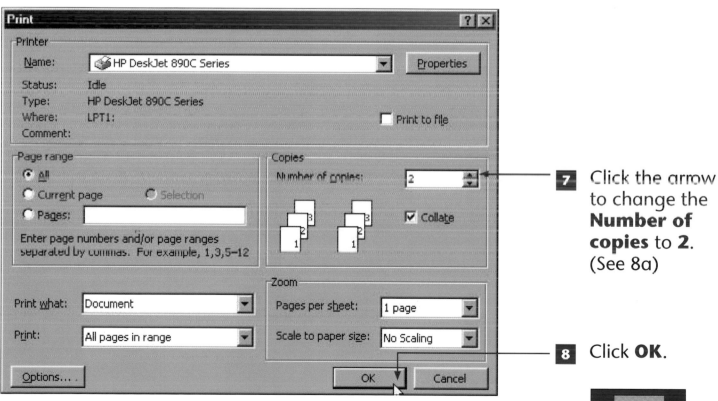

7 Click the arrow to change the **Number of copies** to **2**. (See 8a)

8 Click **OK**.

9 Do this task again but use the icon at the top of the screen. (Go back to **1**)

Print Preview and Print

1 **Open** an existing document.

2 Click **File**.

3 Click **Print Preview**.

*What if I want to change something I see in the **Preview**?*

File	
New...	Ctrl+N
Open...	Ctrl+O
Close	
Save	Ctrl+S
Save As...	
Versions...	
Page Setup...	
Print Preview	
Print...	Ctrl+P
1 Phillip Thomas Picnic List.doc	
2 Kirsty Long - Party List.doc	
3 Jamie Smith - Birthday List.doc	
4 Bethany Easter List.doc	
Exit	

If you are not happy with the way the page looks:

● Click **Close**. `Close`

● Make your changes.

● Click **Print Preview**.
(Go back to **3**)

4 When you are happy with the appearance of the page, click the **Print** icon once to **Print** your work.

Print

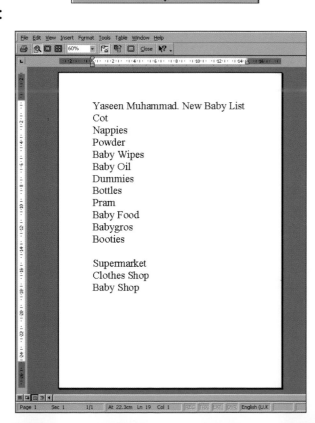

Yaseen Muhammad. New Baby List
Cot
Nappies
Powder
Baby Wipes
Baby Oil
Dummies
Bottles
Pram
Baby Food
Babygros
Booties

Supermarket
Clothes Shop
Baby Shop

Check Work in Print Preview

SKILL: Print Preview and Print

9b

APPLICATION

1 Open a **New** document.

2 Type your first name and surname.

3 Press **Enter**.

4 Type your class name or number.

5 Change the **Font**. (See 5a)

6 Change the **Font Size** to **72**. (See 6a)

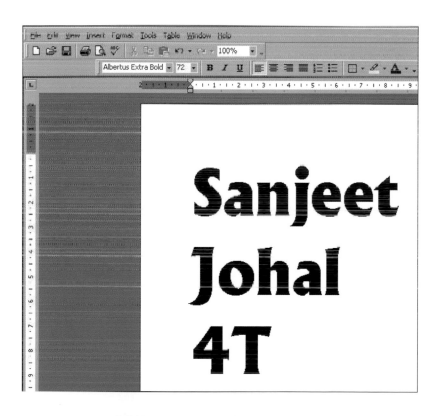

7 **Print Preview** your work. (See 9a)

8 If your name is too big to fit on one line, click **Close**.

9 Change the **Font Size** to **48**.

10 **Print** your work. (See 8a)

11 Do this task again but use the icons at the top of the screen. (Go back to **1**)

Setting-up a Landscape Page

1 Open a **New** document.

2 Click **File**.

3 Click **Page Setup**.

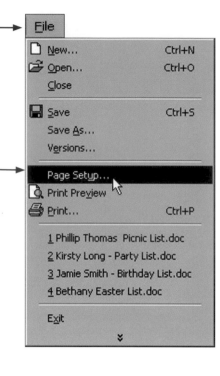

File

New...	Ctrl+N
Open...	Ctrl+O
Close	
Save	Ctrl+S
Save As...	
Versions...	
Page Setup...	
Print Preview	
Print...	Ctrl+P

1 Phillip Thomas Picnic List.doc
2 Kirsty Long - Party List.doc
3 Jamie Smith - Birthday List.doc
4 Bethany Easter List.doc

Exit

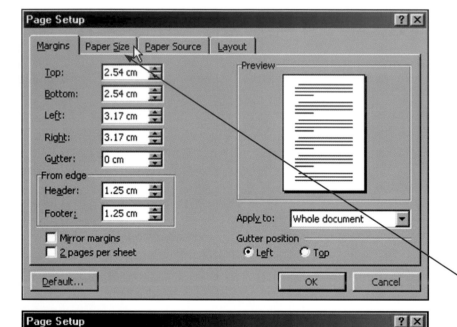

Page Setup

Margins | Paper Size | Paper Source | Layout

Top: 2.54 cm
Bottom: 2.54 cm
Left: 3.17 cm
Right: 3.17 cm
Gutter: 0 cm
From edge
Header: 1.25 cm
Footer: 1.25 cm

Preview

Apply to: Whole document

Mirror margins
2 pages per sheet

Gutter position
Left   Top

Default...   OK   Cancel

4 Click **Paper Size**.

Page Setup

Margins | Paper Size | Paper Source | Layout

Paper size:
A4 (210 x 297 mm)

Width: 29.7 cm
Height: 21 cm

Orientation
A   Portrait
     Landscape

Preview

Apply to: Whole document

Default...   OK   Cancel

5 Click **Landscape**, so that there is a black dot next to it.

6 Click **OK**.

My Favourite Pop Star

SKILL: Setting-up a Landscape Page

1 Open a **New** document.

2 Set-up a **Landscape** page. (See 10a)

3 Click **Font** and select **Arial**. (See 5a)

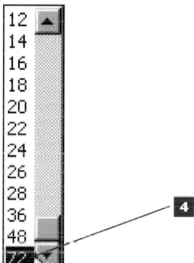

4 Click on **Font Size** and select **72**.

5 Type the name of your favourite pop star.

6 Press **Enter**.

7 Change the **Font Size** to **28**. (See 6a)

8 Write three sentences about why you like them.

9 Check your work in **Print Preview**. (See 9a)

10 **Save** and **Print** your work.

My Favourite Pop Star

I like all the songs on the album. She has good dance moves. she has beautiful hair.

Using Bold

Making text stand out by using Bold

1 Open a **New** document.

2 Click the letter **B**. This is the **Bold** icon.

When you type, the text will appear in **Bold.**

*What if I want to make my words **Bold** after I have typed them?*

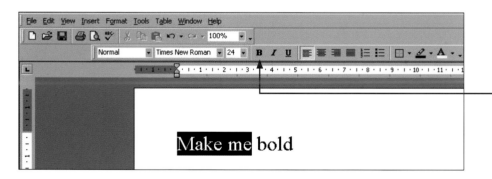

Make me bold

● **Highlight** your text by dragging the I over it, holding down the left mouse button.

● Click the **Bold** icon and the words will become **Bold**.

● Click anywhere on the screen.

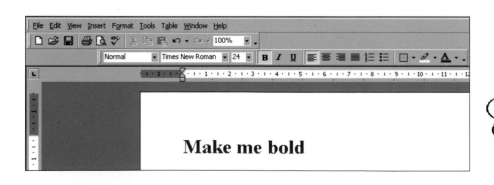

Make me bold

*Remember This will not work unless you **Highlight** the text first.*

WordWorks

© Folens (non-copiable)

1 Open a **New** document.

2 Click the **Bold** icon.

3 Type the title of your favourite book.

4 Press **Enter**.

5 Click the **Bold** icon to change the **Font** to normal.

6 Write three sentences about why you like the book.

7 **Save** your work.

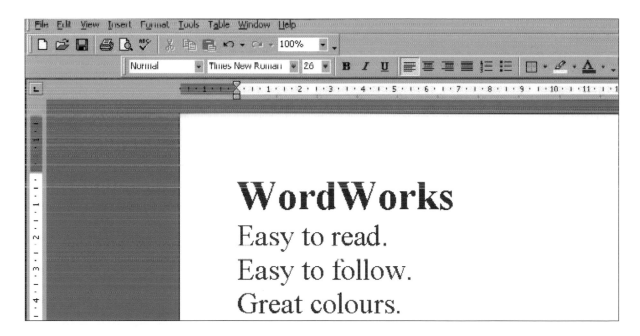

8 Check your work in **Print Preview**. (See 9a)

9 **Print** your work.

Changing your text to Italic

1 Open a **New** document.

2 Click the letter **I**. This is the **Italic** icon.

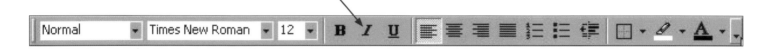

When you type, the text will appear in **Italic.**

*What if I want to make my words **Italic** after I have typed them?*

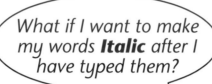

Make me Italic

- **Highlight** your text by dragging the I over it, holding down the left mouse button.

- Click the **Italic** icon.

- Click anywhere on the screen.

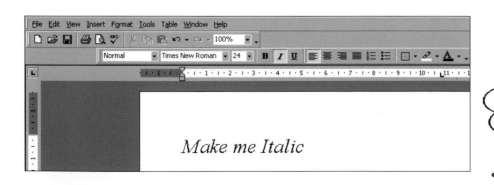

Make me Italic

*__Remember__ This will not work unless you **Highlight** the text first.*

12b

APPLICATION

1 Open a **New** document.

2 Type the sentences in the box below.
Add three examples to each sentence in *Italic*. (See 12a)
The first one is done for you.

● Lots of people go abroad on holiday, for example to *Spain, India, Australia.*

● I eat fruit, for example

● I like healthy food, for example

● Farms have different animals, for example

● There are many makes of car, for example

---

3 Add three sentences of your own.

4 **Save** and **Print** your work.
(See 8a)

Underlining

Underlining your work

1 Open a **New** document.

2 Click the letter **U**. This is the **Underline** icon.

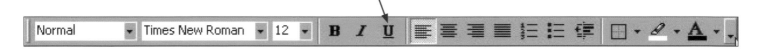

When you type, the text will appear **Underlined**.

What if I want to **Underline** *words after I have typed them?*

● **Highlight** the words you want to **Underline** by dragging the I over them, holding down the left mouse button.

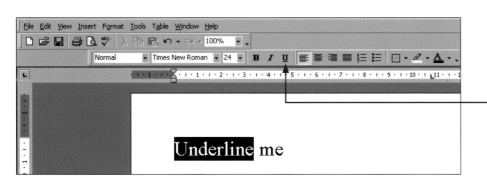

● Click the **Underline** icon.

● Click anywhere on the screen.

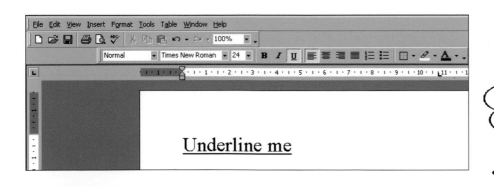

Remember
This will not work unless you **Highlight** *the words first.*

WordWorks

Multiples of 2

SKILL: Underlining

1 Open a **New** document.

2 Type the following numbers.
Underline the numbers that are multiples of 2. (See 13a)

1	6	11	16
2	7	12	17
3	8	13	18
4	9	14	19
5	10	15	20

3 **Save** and **Print** your work.

Aligning Text

Align your text

1 Open a **New** document.

2 Find the **Align** icons on your screen.

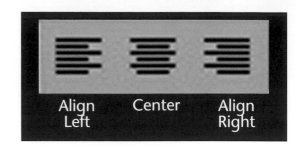

Align Left   Center   Align Right

3 Click the **Align Right** icon.

Type 'Align Right'

4 Click the **Align Left** icon.

Type 'Align Left'

5 Click the **Center** (**Centre**) icon.

Type 'Centre'

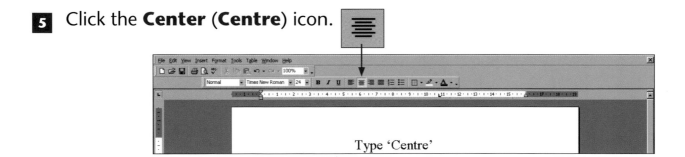

*You can **Align** a single line of text if your cursor is on the line. If you want to **Align** a page of text, highlight the words that you want to **Align** and click the **Align** icon of your choice.*

WordWorks

Use Align Icons

SKILL: Aligning Text

14b

APPLICATION

1 Open a **New** document.

2 Type the following words:

Right-hand side

3 Click the **Align Right** icon.

The words will now move to the right side of your screen.

4 Press **Enter**.

5 Type:

Left-hand side

6 Click the **Align Left** icon.

The words will now move to the left side of your screen.

7 Press **Enter**.

8 Type:

Centre

9 Click the **Center** (**Centre**) icon.

The word 'Centre' will move to the middle of your screen.

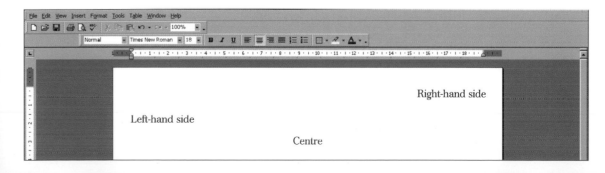

10 **Save** and **Print** your work.

Highlighting Text in Colour

Highlighting *can be done only to words that you have typed already.*

1 **Open** a File that you have already worked on.

2 **Highlight** your text by dragging the I over it, holding down the left mouse button.

3 To see the choice of colours, click the arrow right of the **Highlight** icon.

4 Move the mouse pointer around on the colours and a box will tell you what the colours are.

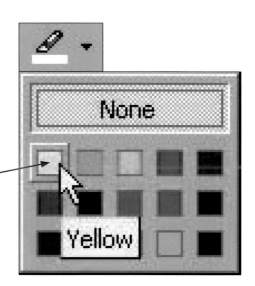

5 Click the colour you want.

The word will now be **Highlighted** in that colour.

6 Try different colours.

7 When you are happy with the colour, click anywhere on the screen.

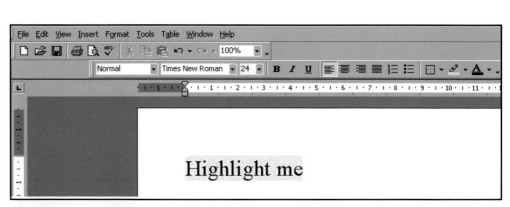

1 Open a **New** document.

2 Type your full name.

3 Press **Enter**.

4 Type your class name or number.

5 **Highlight** your name in yellow. (See 15a)

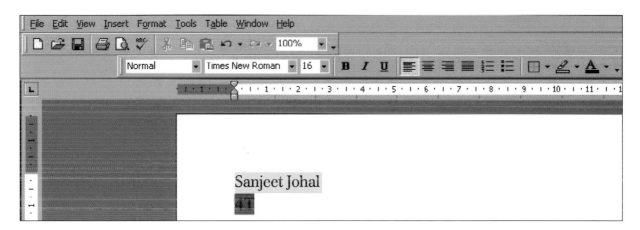

6 **Highlight** your class name or number in purple.

7 Now type a list of your best friends.
Remember to press **Enter** after each name.

8 **Highlight** the girls in green and
the boys in grey .

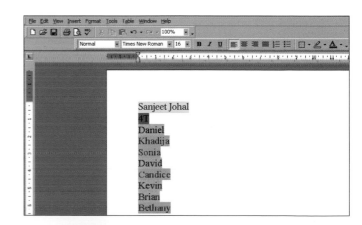

9 **Save** and **Print**.

Format Font – Changing Font

1 Open a **New** document.

2 Click **Format**.

3 Click **Font**.

The **Font** screen will now appear.

4 Click the **Font** tab.

5 Click the **Font** you want.

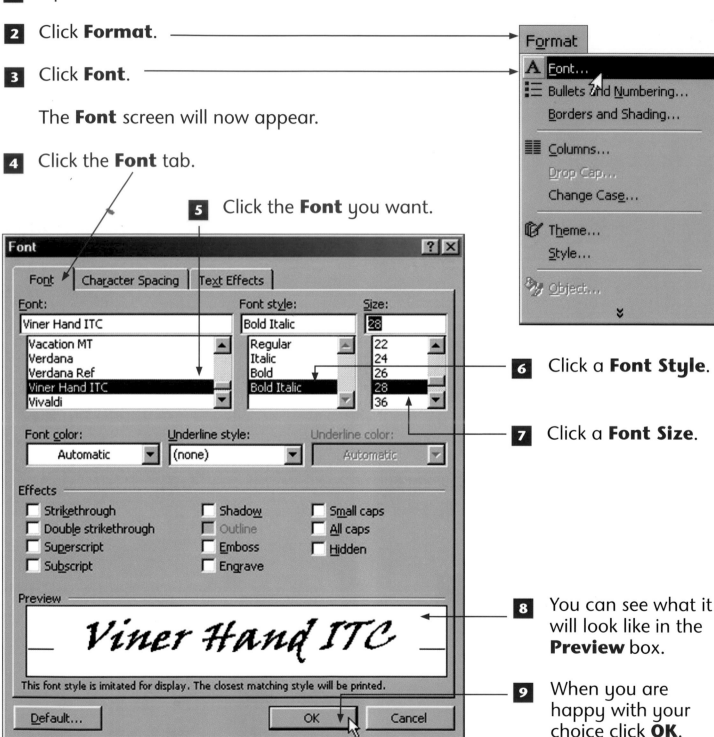

6 Click a **Font Style**.

7 Click a **Font Size**.

8 You can see what it will look like in the **Preview** box.

9 When you are happy with your choice click **OK**.

Experiment with Fonts

APPLICATION

SKILL: Format Font – Changing Font

1 Open a **New** document.

2 Use **Format Font** to type the following words using a different **Font**, **Font Style** and **Font Size** for each. (See 16a)

For example, 'Scary Tiger' could be written as: **Scary Tiger**

Or 'Curly Hair' could be written as: Curly Hair

- Roman Soldier
- Computer
- Secret Diary
- Big Mountain
- Spooky Forest
- Squeaky Mouse
- Heavy Books

- Mischievous Monkeys
- Fountain Pen
- Christmas Party

3 **Save** and **Print**.

Format Font – Colour and Underlining

Changing Font colour and Underline style

1 Open a **New** document.

2 Click **Format**.

3 Click **Font**.

The **Font** window will now appear.

4 Click the **Font** tab.

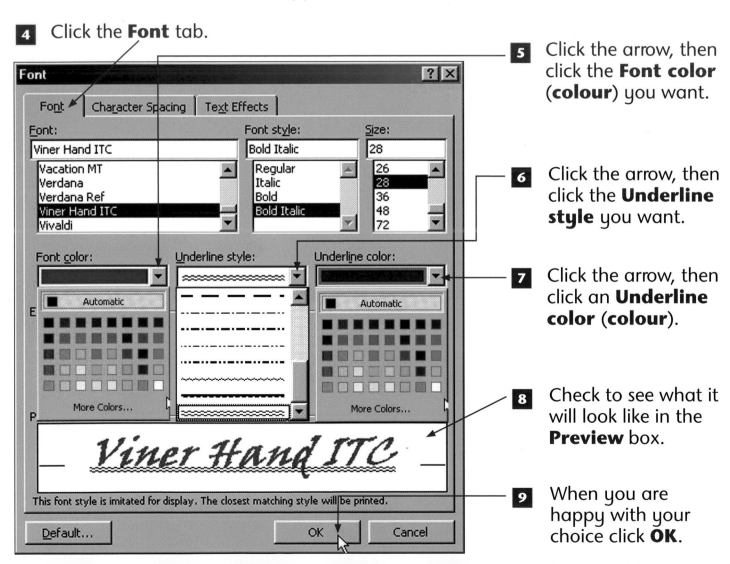

5 Click the arrow, then click the **Font color (colour)** you want.

6 Click the arrow, then click the **Underline style** you want.

7 Click the arrow, then click an **Underline color (colour)**.

8 Check to see what it will look like in the **Preview** box.

9 When you are happy with your choice click **OK**.

1 Open a **New** document.

2 Set-up a **Landscape** page. (See 10a)

3 Use **Format Font** to create a 'Keep Out' sign for your bedroom.
 (See 16a and 17a)

- Think about what type of **Font** you want. Does it suit your personality?
- Think about **Font style**. Does it need to be **Bold** or in *Italic*?
- Think about **Font size**. Will it all fit on an A4 page?
- Think about **Font colour**.
- Think about **Underline style** and **Underline colour**.

---

4 **Centre** your work.
(See 14a)

5 Use **Print Preview**
to check that you
are happy with
your work.
You might want to
change the **Font**,
Size or **Colour** of
the text.

6 **Save** and **Print**.

Choosing Effects

1 Open a **New** document.

2 Click **Format**.

3 Click **Font**.

The **Font** window will now appear.

4 Click the **Font** tab.

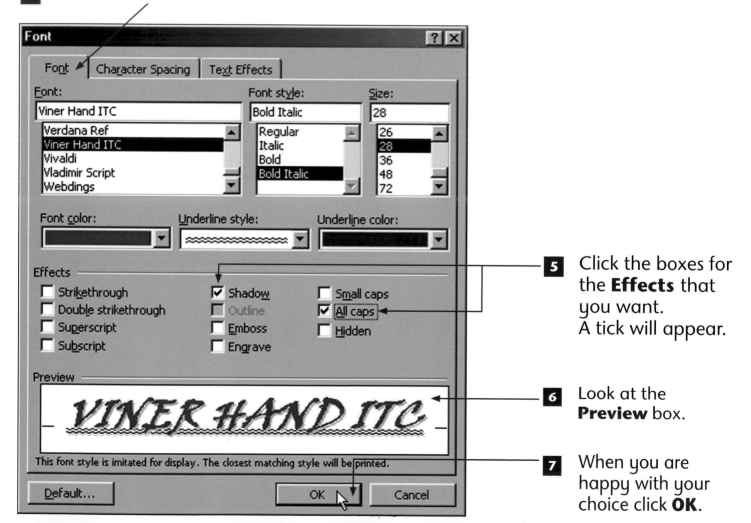

5 Click the boxes for the **Effects** that you want. A tick will appear.

6 Look at the **Preview** box.

7 When you are happy with your choice click **OK**.

Explore Font Effects

SKILL: Format Font – Using Effects

1 Open a **New** document.

2 Type the following words using the matching **Format Font Effect** for each. (See 18a)

- Strikethrough
- Double strikethrough
- Superscript
- Subscript
- Shadow
- Outline
- Emboss
- Engrave
- Small caps
- All caps

3 Change the **Font, Style, Size** and **Colour** of each. (See 16a and 17a)

4 **Save** and **Print**.

19a SKILL

Undo Typing

1 Open a **New** document.

2 Type your name.

3 Click **Edit**.

4 Click **Undo Typing**.

Your name will disappear because **Undo Typing** will cancel what you did last.

*I can use this to **Undo** my mistakes.*

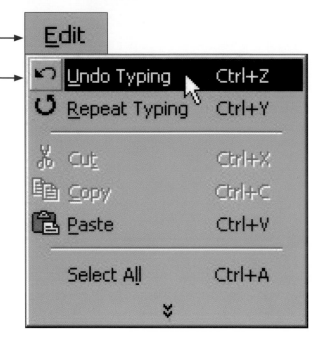

Redo Typing

5 Click **Edit**.

6 Click **Redo Typing**.

Your name will now reappear.

*I can use this if I pressed **Undo** by mistake.*

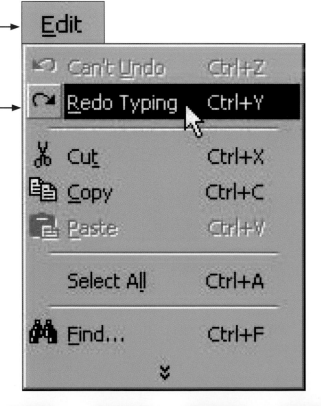

Use Undo and Redo

SKILL: Undo and Redo

1 Open a **New** document.

2 Type your first name.

3 Change the **Font Size**.

4 Change the **Font**.

5 **Underline** your name. (See 13a or 17a)

6 Change the **Font Colour** of each of the letters. (See 7a or 17a)

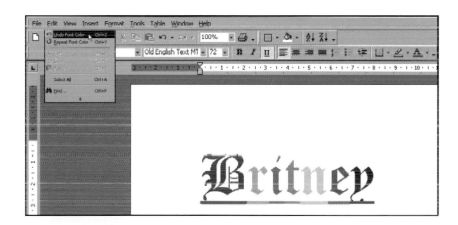

7 Click **Edit – Undo**.
Count how many clicks
it takes to get back to a
blank page.
(See 19a)

8 Click **Edit – Redo** to
check your answer.
(See 19a)

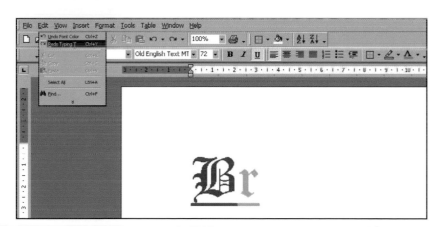

9 Do this task again but
use the icons at the top
of the screen.
(Go back to **1**)

Copy and Paste

Copy

1 Open a **New** document.

2 Type some words.

3 **Highlight** the words you want to copy.

4 Click **Edit.**

5 Click **Copy.**

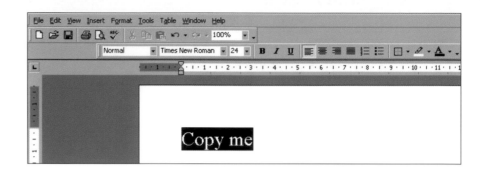

Paste

6 Click **Edit.**

7 Click **Paste.**

Your words will now be **Pasted** on the page.

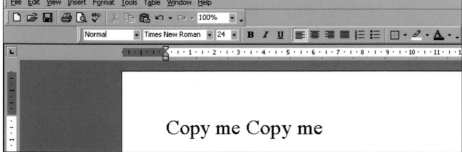

Keep Out Sign

SKILL: Copy and Paste

APPLICATION

Your best friends like the design of your 'Keep Out' sign and would like you to make some for them.

1 **Open** the File that you saved your 'Keep Out' sign in. (See 17b)

2 **Highlight** the words 'Keep Out!'.

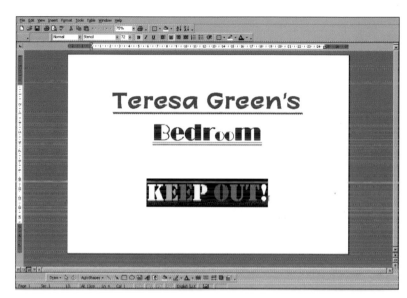

3 **Copy** the words. (See 20a)

4 Open a **New** document.

5 Set-up a **Landscape** page. (See 10a)

6 **Paste** the words. (See 20a)

7 Add your friend's details.

8 **Save** and **Print**.

Cut and Paste

Cut

1 Open a **New** document.

2 Type some words.

3 **Highlight** the words you want to **Cut**.

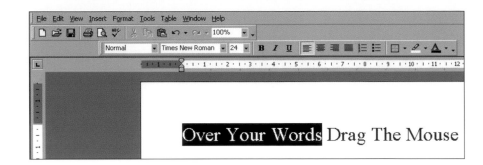

4 Click **Edit**. ————————————————→

5 Click **Cut**. ————————————————→

Paste

6 Click where you want to **Paste** the words.

7 Click **Edit**. ————————→

8 Click **Paste**.

Your words will now be **Pasted** in the correct place.

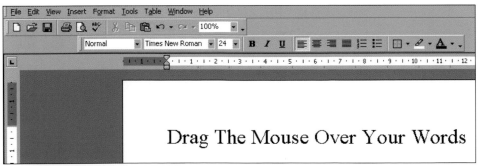

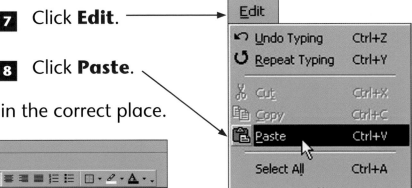

WordWorks

1 Open a **New** document.

2 Type the following:

one	A hexagon has this many sides
three	A square has this many sides
four	A triangle has this many sides
six	An octagon has this many sides
eight	A circle has this many sides

3 **Cut** and **Paste** the correct answers next to where they should go. (See 21a)

4 Do this activity again using these icons. (Go back to **1**)

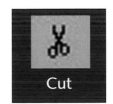

Cut

Paste

5 **Save**.

22a

SKILL

Using Select All

1 Open a **New** document.

2 Type some words.

3 Click **Edit**.

4 Click **Select All**.

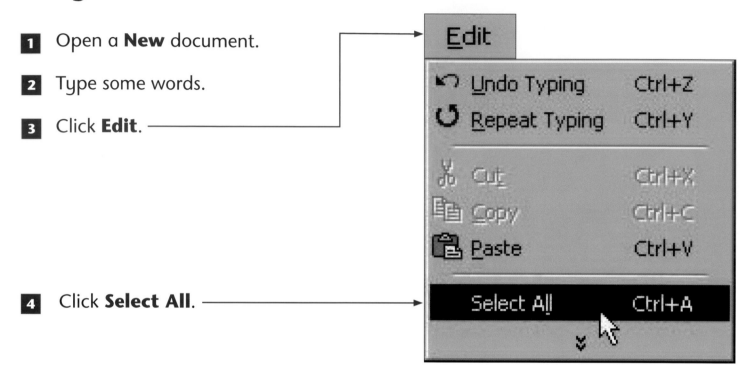

Everything on your page will now be selected.

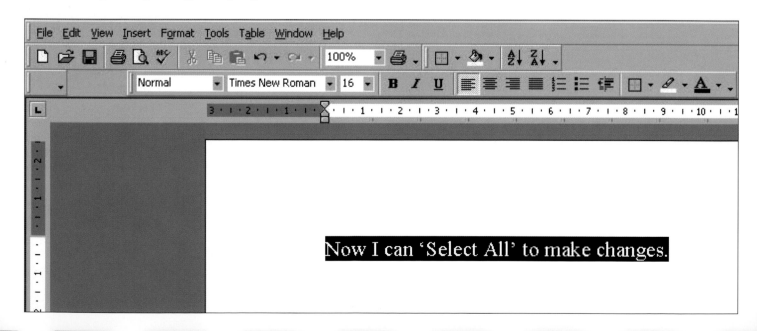

Now I can 'Select All' to make changes.

Design a Poster

SKILL: Using Select All

APPLICATION

1 **Open** the document that you saved for your non-uniform day. (CD activity 17.1)

2 **Highlight** all the text using **Select All**. (See 22a)

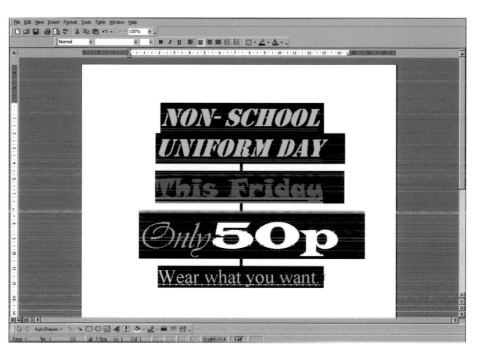

3 **Copy** the text. (See 20a)

4 Open a **New** document.

5 **Paste** the poster in the new document.

6 Change the word 'Friday' to 'Thursday'.

7 Redesign the poster.

8 **Save** and **Print**.

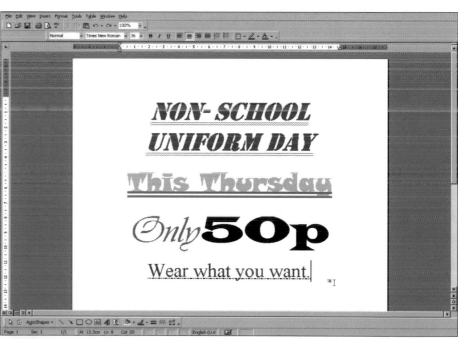

Find and Replace

1 Open a **New** document.

2 Type in some words.

3 Click **Edit**. ─────────────

4 Click **Find**. ─────────────

A **Find and Replace** box will appear.

5 Click the **Replace** tab.

Edit	
↶ Undo Typing	Ctrl+Z
↻ Repeat Typing	Ctrl+Y
✂ Cut	Ctrl+X
▤ Copy	Ctrl+C
▣ Paste	Ctrl+V
Select All	Ctrl+A
🔍 Find...	Ctrl+F

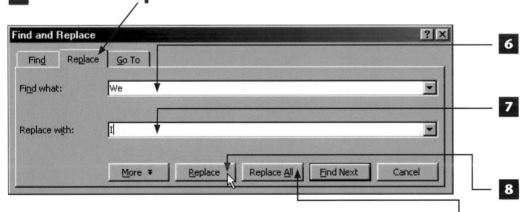

6 Type the word that you want to **Find**.

7 Type the word that you want to **Replace** it with.

8 Click **Replace** to change the words one by one.

OR

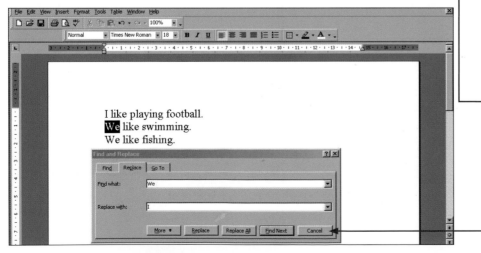

9 Click **Replace All** to change the words everywhere they appear in the document.

10 Click **Cancel** if you want to stop.

1 Open a **New** document.

2 Type the following:

> ## She sells sea shells on the sea shore.

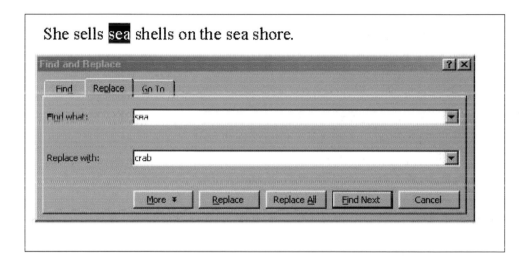

3 **Find** the first 'sea' and **Replace** it with the word 'crab' by clicking **Replace**. (See 23a)

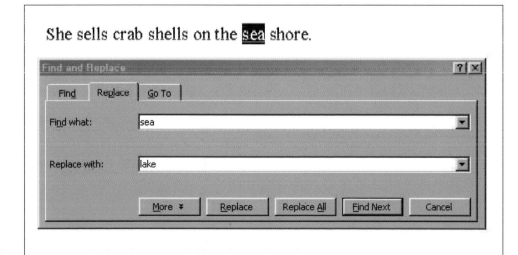

4 **Replace** the second 'sea' with the word 'lake'.

5 **Save**.

24a

Using Headers and Footers

SKILL

Headers

1 Open a **New** document.

2 Click **View**.

3 Click **Header and Footer**.

4 Type your **Header** in the **Header** box.

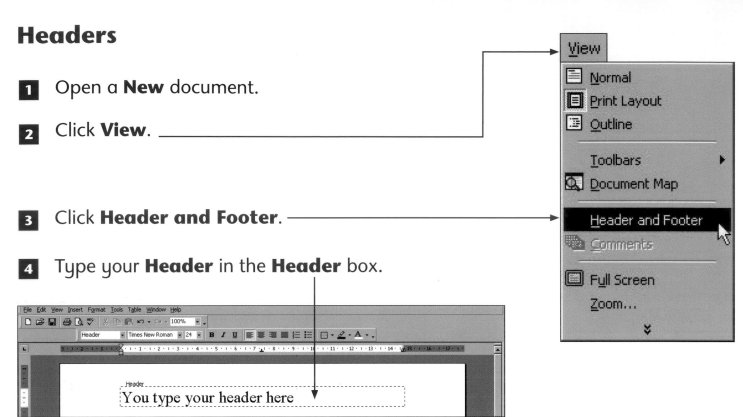

5 Click the **Switch Between Header and Footer** icon.

Footers

The **Footer** box will now show.

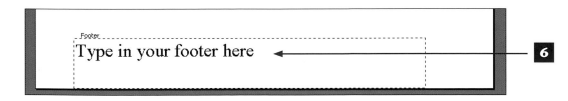

6 Type your **Footer** in the **Footer** box.

WordWorks

School Play Leaflet

SKILL: Using Headers and Footers

24b

APPLICATION

1 Open a **New** document.

2 Design a leaflet advertising a school play.

3 Make sure the leaflet contains:

- Title of play
- Where the play is going to be held
- Date of performance
- Time of performance.

*Think about **Font**, **Style**, **Size** and **Colour** of the text.*

4 Add a **Header** to the leaflet, this can be the name of your school. (See 24a)

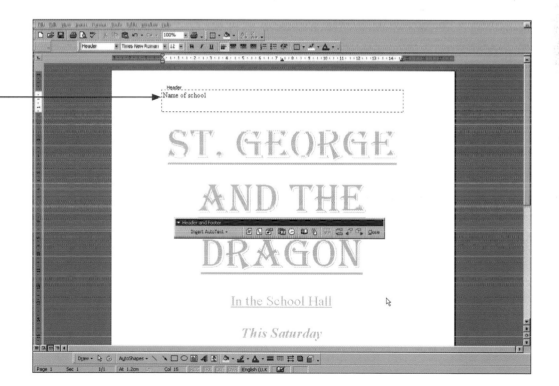

5 Add the **Footer** 'Designed by' and your name.

6 Check your work in **Print Preview**.

7 **Save** and **Print**.

25a

SKILL

1 Open a **New** document.

2 Click **Insert**. ───────────────────

3 Click **Break**. ───────────────────

The **Break** box will appear.

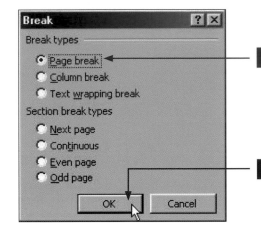

4 Click **Page break** if there is no black dot.

Insert

Break...

Page Numbers...

Field...

Picture ▶

Object...

5 Click **OK**.

You will now be ready to start at the top of the next page.

What if I have already typed text that I want to move to a new page?

● Click the **I** at the beginning of the text where you would like your next page to start.
(Go back to **2**)

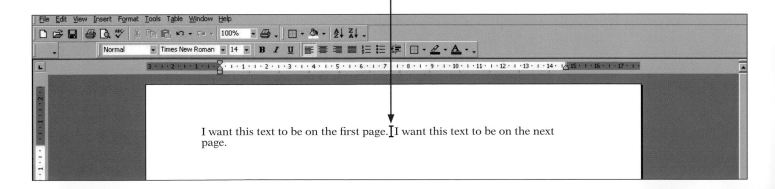

1 Open a **New** document.

2 Type the following:

Page 1	Page 6
Page 2	Page 7
Page 3	Page 8
Page 4	Page 9
Page 5	Page 10

3 You may want to change the **Font**, **Style**, **Size** or **Colour** of each.

4 Insert **Page breaks** so that each page number starts a new page. For example, 'Page 1' will be at the top of the first page and 'Page 2' will be at the top of the second page. (See 25a)

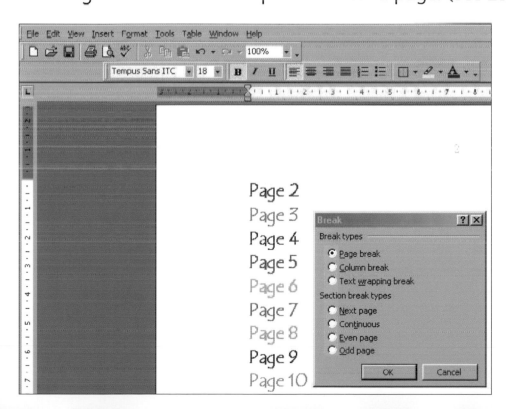

5 Save.

It is important to **Save** this File; you will be using it again.

Inserting Page Numbers

1 Open a **New** document.

2 Click **Insert**.

3 Click **Page Numbers**.

The **Page Numbers** box will appear.

> Insert
> Break...
> Page Numbers...
> Field...
> Picture ▶
> Object...
> ⌄

4 Click the **Position** arrow.

> **Page Numbers** ? X
> Position:
> Bottom of page (Footer) ▼
> Top of page (Header)
> Bottom of page (Footer)
> Right ▼
> ☑ Show number on first page
> Preview
> OK   Cancel   Format...

5 Click whether you want the **Page Numbers** at the top or bottom of the page.

6 Click the **Alignment** arrow.

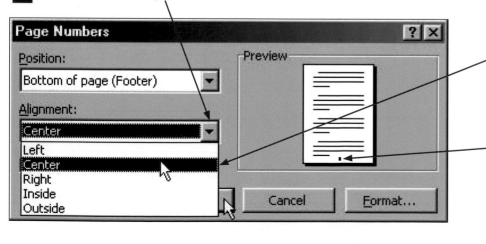

> **Page Numbers** ? X
> Position:
> Bottom of page (Footer) ▼
> Alignment:
> Center ▼
> Left
> Center
> Right
> Inside
> Outside
> Preview
> Cancel   Format...

7 Click where you want the **Page Numbers** to appear.

8 **Preview** where the **Page Number** will appear on the page.

9 Click **OK**.

Jokes

SKILL: Inserting Page Numbers

1 Open a **New** document.

2 Set-up a **Landscape** page.

3 Set the **Font Size** to **48** and choose a **Font**.

4 Type the following:

> # Why do cows have bells?

5 Insert a **Page break**. (See 25a)

6 Type the following using a different **Font Colour**. (See 7a)

> # Because their horns don't work.

7 Insert **Page Numbers**. (See 26a)

8 **Save** and **Print**.

Try this exercise using two of your own jokes. Type the question on one page and the answer on the other.
(Go back to **1**)

Inserting AutoText

Using AutoText to help write letters

1 Open a **New** document.

2 Click **Insert**.

3 Click **AutoText**.

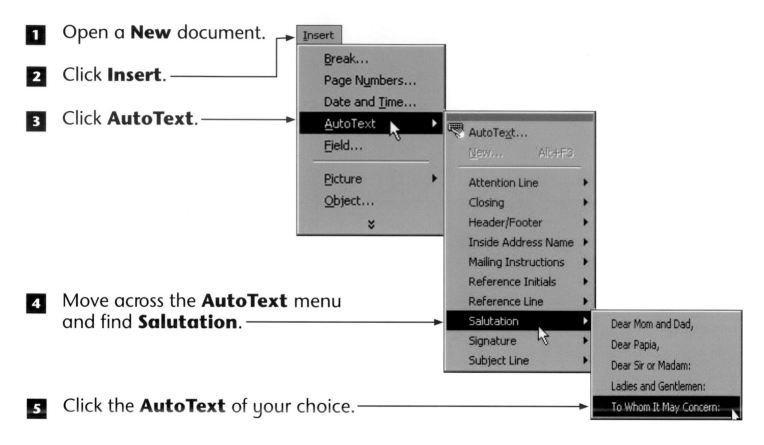

4 Move across the **AutoText** menu and find **Salutation**.

5 Click the **AutoText** of your choice.

6 Repeat the process to pick a **Closing** phrase. (Go back to **2**)

Your chosen **AutoText** will now be inserted onto your page.

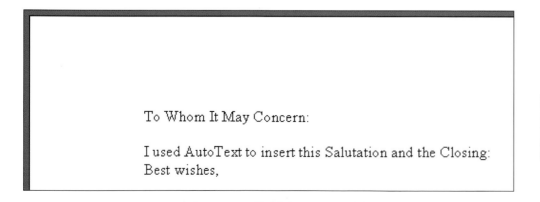

To Whom It May Concern:

I used AutoText to insert this Salutation and the Closing:
Best wishes,

I can now add words without typing.

1 Open a **New** document.

2 Use **AutoText** and type the blue text. (See 27a)

Reference: 27b   (Use Reference Line)

Subject: School Dinners   (Use Subject Line)

CONFIDENTIAL   (Use Mailing Instructions)

Dear Sir or Madam,   (Use Salutation)
Thank you for making our school dinners, I especially love the puddings.
Regards,   (Use Closing)

Type your name here.

Reference: 27b

Subject: School Dinners

CONFIDENTIAL

Dear Sir or Madam,
Thank you for making our school dinners, I especially love the puddings.
Regards,

Melissa Martin

---

3 **Save** and **Print**.

28a

SKILL

Inserting Symbols

1 Open a **New** document.

2 Click **Insert**.

3 Click **Symbol**.

The **Symbol** box will appear.

4 Click the **Symbol** tab.

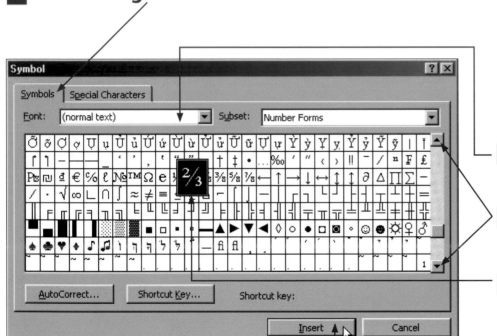

5 Make sure the **Font** is set to (normal text).

6 Click the arrows to see the **Symbols**.

7 Click the **Symbol** that you want to insert.

8 Click **Insert**.

9 Click **Close**.

*Now I can add **Symbols** to my work that are not on my keyboard.*

Select Symbols

APPLICATION

1 Type the following sentences.

Diamonds are a girl's best friend.

I ate half a cake for my lunch.

It was a sunny day.

I enjoy listening to music.

I love my dog.

When I finish my homework, my teacher puts a tick on the page.

Jokes make me smile.

2 Choose and insert a **Symbol** for each sentence. (See 28a)

The first one is done for you.

3 Insert the following **Symbols** and write a sentence to match each one.

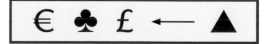

4 **Save** and **Print**.

WordWorks

Add a File to your work

1 Open a **New** document.

2 Click **Insert**.

3 Click **File**.

The **Insert File** box will appear.

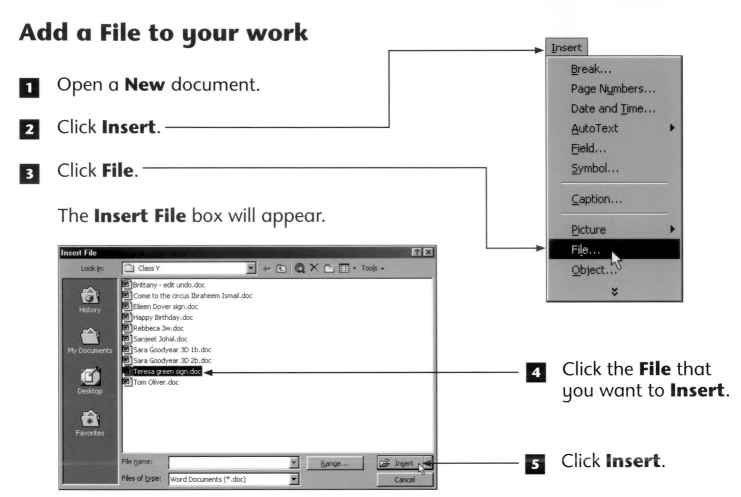

4 Click the **File** that you want to **Insert**.

5 Click **Insert**.

The **File** will now be **Inserted** into your new document.

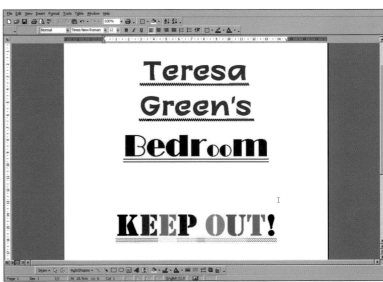

Change the Pyjama Poster

SKILL: Inserting a File

1 Open a **New** document.

2 **Insert** the **File** that you saved for the pyjama poster. (CD activity 18.1) (See 29a)

Stripy Pyjamas

With five bright colours

Red Stripe

Blue Stripe

GREEN STRIPE

Yellow Stripe

AND ORANGE STRIPE

In Stock Now

3 Change the word 'five' to 'six'.

Stripy Pyjamas

With six bright colours

Red Stripe

Blue Stripe

GREEN STRIPE

Yellow Stripe

ORANGE STRIPE

And Turquoise Stripe

In Stock Now

4 Add a colour stripe of your choice, using **Format Font**.

5 **Save** and **Print**.

Inserting ClipArt

Inserting pictures

1 Open a **New** document.

2 Click **Insert**.

3 Move to **Picture**.

The **Insert ClipArt** box will appear.

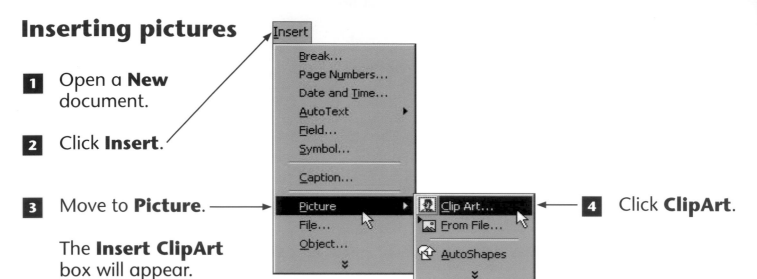

4 Click **ClipArt**.

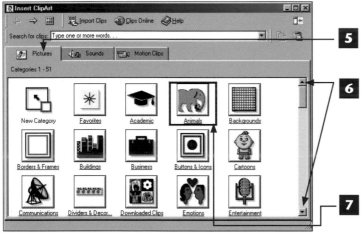

5 Click the **Pictures** tab.

6 Use the arrows to see all the **Categories**.

7 Click the **Category** of **Picture** that you want.

8 Click the **Picture** that you want.

9 Click the **Insert Clip** icon.

The **ClipArt** will now be inserted on your page.

10 Click the cross in the top right-hand corner to close **ClipArt**.

My Pet

SKILL: Inserting ClipArt

1   Open a **New** document.

2   If you have a pet type:

> 'My pet is a '

> My pet is a

If you don't have a pet type:

> 'The kind of pet I would like is a '

> The kind of pet I would like is a

3   Press **Enter**.

4   Insert a **ClipArt** picture of the kind of pet you have or would like. (See 30a)

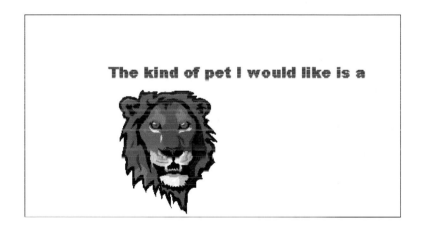

5   **Save** and **Print**.

6   Try this again using the **ClipArt** icon at the bottom of the screen.
(Go back **1**)

Moving and Resizing

Moving Objects

> **ClipArt** *and other drawn objects can be moved around on the page.*

1 Open a **New** document.

2 Insert **ClipArt** on your page. (See 30a)

3 To move the object: click, hold and move the shape using ⬌ .

4 When it is in the correct place, let go of the mouse.

Resizing Objects

5 Click the object so that you can see small boxes around it.

6 Move the cursor to one of the boxes around the shape, until it turns into ↗ .

7 Click and drag until the object is the size that you want.

8 When you are happy with the position and size, click anywhere on the page.

> **Remember**
> *Pull outwards to make the shape bigger.*
> *Push inwards to make it smaller.*

WordWorks

Arranging ClipArt

SKILL: Moving and Resizing

1 Open a **New** document.

2 Insert six **ClipArt** pictures of your choice onto the same page. (See 30a)

3 You will need to **Resize** and **Move** the pictures so that all six fill one page. (See 31a)

4 Check your work in **Print Preview**.

5 **Save** and **Print**.

To move between **Categories** use the **Back** and **Forward** arrows.

Back

Forward

Inserting Pictures from a CD

SKILL

1 Open a **New** document.

2 Click **Insert**.

*You will need any CD with **Pictures**.*

3 Move to **Picture**.

Insert
- Break...
- Page Numbers...
- Date and Time...
- AutoText ▶
- Field...
- Symbol...
- Caption...
- Picture ▶
  - Clip Art...
  - From File...
  - AutoShapes
  - WordArt...
  - From Scanner or Camera...
  - Chart
- Text Box
- File...

4 Click **From File**.

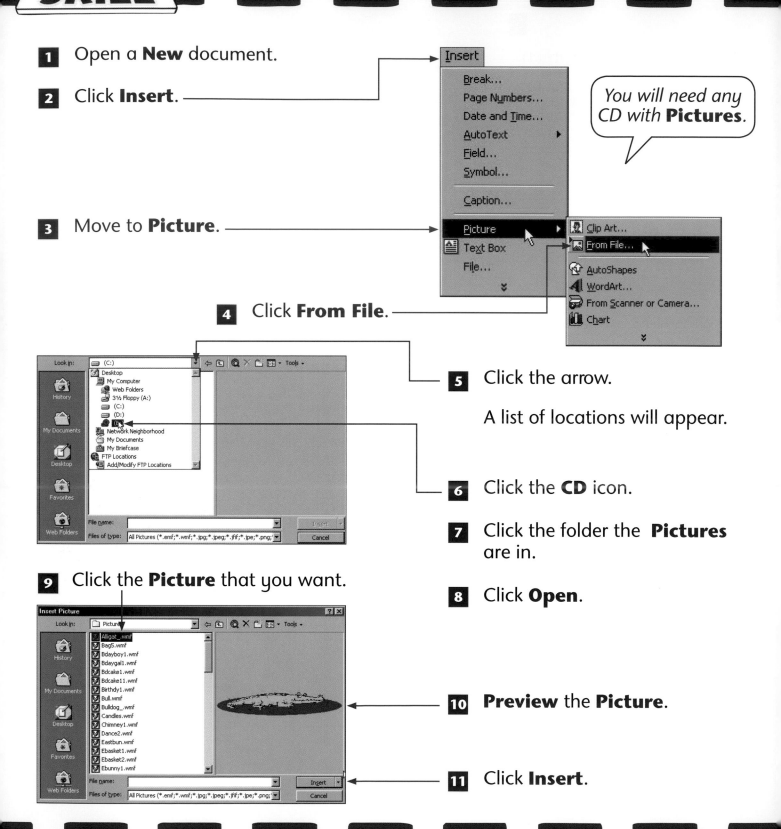

5 Click the arrow.

A list of locations will appear.

6 Click the **CD** icon.

7 Click the folder the **Pictures** are in.

9 Click the **Picture** that you want.

8 Click **Open**.

10 **Preview** the **Picture**.

11 Click **Insert**.

Find the Pictures

SKILL: Inserting Pictures from a CD

1 Open a **New** document.

2 Insert four **Pictures** of young animals using a CD. (See 32a)

3 Label each **Picture**. Here are some examples.

Lynx cub

Wolf cubs

Fox cubs

Seal pup

4 **Resize** the **Pictures** if necessary. (See 31a)

5 **Save** and **Print**.

33a

SKILL

1 Open a **New** document.

2 Click **Insert**.

3 Move to **Picture**.

4 Click **WordArt**.

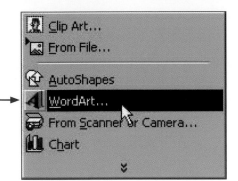

- Clip Art...
- From File...
- AutoShapes
- WordArt...
- From Scanner or Camera...
- Chart

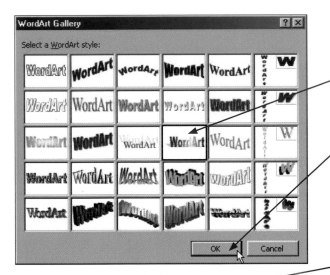

WordArt Gallery

Select a WordArt style:

5 Click the **WordArt** you want.

6 Click **OK**.

7 Type your text.

8 Click **OK**.

9 **Move** or **Resize** the **WordArt**. (See 31a)

10 Click anywhere on the page when you are finished.

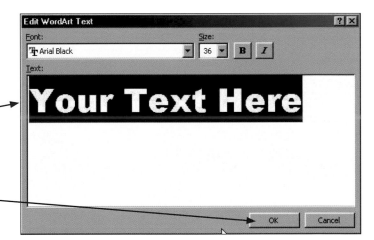

Edit WordArt Text

Font: Arial Black   Size: 36   **B** *I*

Text:

Your Text Here

What if I change my mind and want to type something else?

- Double-click on the **WordArt** to change the text.

1 Open a **New** document.

2 Use the **WordArt** gallery. (See 33a)

3 Select the best styles to recreate these words:

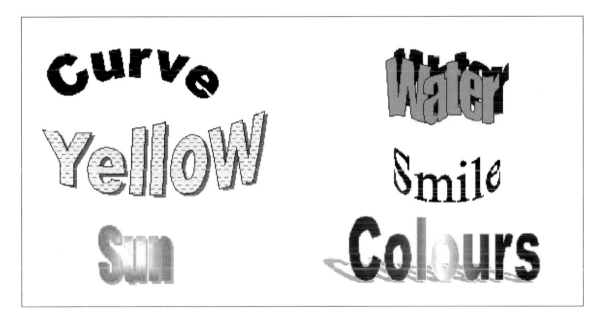

Remember
*After you have inserted **WordArt**, click anywhere on the screen.*
*If you have boxes around your **WordArt** you can't insert any*
*more **WordArt** or **ClipArt**.*

4 Check your work in **Print Preview**.

5 **Save** and **Print**.

6 Try this again using the **WordArt** icon. (Go back to **1**)

WordArt

Inserting a Text Box

1 Open a **New** document.

2 Click **Insert**.

3 Click **Text Box**.

4 Click and hold the mouse button where you want your box to start.

5 **Drag** to where you want the box to end and let go of the mouse button.

6 Type your text.

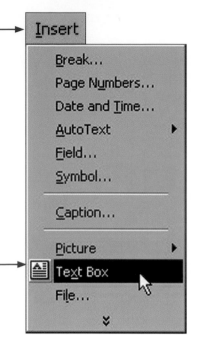

Insert

Break...
Page Numbers...
Date and Time...
AutoText ▶
Field...
Symbol...

Caption...

Picture ▶
Text Box
File...
⋁

Type your text here

7 Click anywhere on the screen when you have finished.

Remember
You can **Resize** or **Move** the **Text Box** after you have typed. You can click in the box after you have typed to change your words. You can also change the **Font**, **Style**, **Size** or **Colour** of the text in the **Text Box**.

WordWorks

Name Tags

SKILL: Inserting a Text Box

34b

APPLICATION

1 Open a **New** document.

2 Insert a **Text Box**. (See 34a)

3 Type the name of someone in your class.

4 You might want to change the **Font**, **Style**, **Size** or **Colour** of the text to suit their personality.

5 You might need to **Resize** your **Text Box**.

6 Check your work in **Print Preview**.

7 **Save** and **Print**.

Inserting AutoShapes

1 Open a **New** document.

2 Click **Insert**.

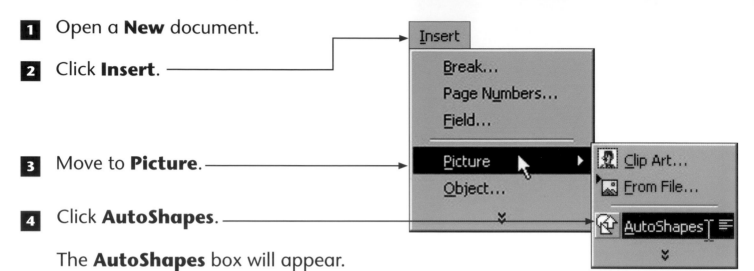

3 Move to **Picture**.

4 Click **AutoShapes**.

The **AutoShapes** box will appear.

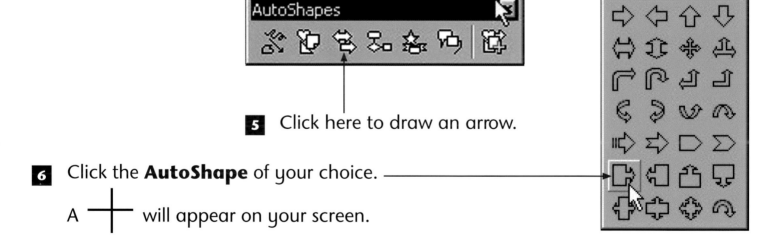

5 Click here to draw an arrow.

6 Click the **AutoShape** of your choice.

A ┼ will appear on your screen.

7 To draw your **AutoShape**, click and hold the mouse button where you want your **AutoShape** to start.

8 Move to where you want the **AutoShape** to end and let go of the mouse button.

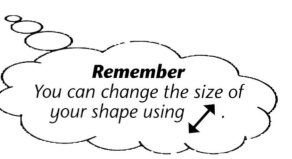

Remember
You can change the size of your shape using ↗.

1 Open a **New** document.

2 Insert the following **AutoShapes** onto one page. (See 35a)

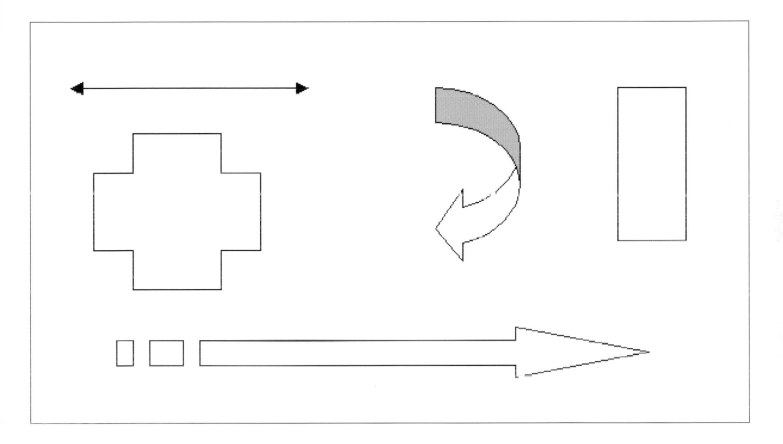

3 **Save** and **Print**.

Inserting Callouts

1 Open a **New** document.

2 Click **Insert**.

3 Move to **Picture**.

4 Click **AutoShapes**.

5 Click the **Callouts** icon.

Insert

| Break... |
| Page Numbers... |
| Field... |
| Picture ▶ |
| Object... |

| Clip Art... |
| From File... |
| AutoShapes |

Callout

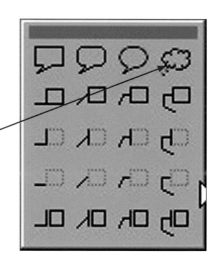

6 Click a **Callout** that you want to use.

7 Click and hold the mouse button where you want your **Callout** to start.

8 Drag to where you want the **Callout** to end and let go of the mouse button.

9 Type the words you want inside your **Callout**.

Remember
*You can change the **Font**, **Style**, **Size** or **Colour** of the text in a **Callout**.*

Jokes Using Callouts

SKILL: Inserting Callouts

36b

APPLICATION

1 Open a **New** document.

2 Set-up a **Landscape** page.

3 Use one of the following jokes.

> **Q** How does a turkey eat its food?
>   **A** It gobbles it up!
>
> **Q** What is the most dangerous vegetable to have on a boat?
>   **A** A leek!
>
> **Q** What did one pencil say to another?
>   **A** You're looking sharp!

4 Insert a **ClipArt** for the question.

5 Insert a **ClipArt** for the answer.

6 Insert **Callouts** for the speech. (See 36a)

7 Check your work in **Print Preview**.

8 **Save** and **Print**.

9 Try this with one of your own jokes.
(Go back to **1**)

37a SKILL

1 Open a **New** document.

2 Click **Format**.

3 Click **Bullets** and **Numbering**.

4 Click the **Bulleted** tab.

Format
- **A** Font...
- **≡** Bullets and Numbering...
- Borders and Shading...
- **≣** Columns...
- Drop Cap...
- **☞** Theme...
- Style...
- **⚙** Object...

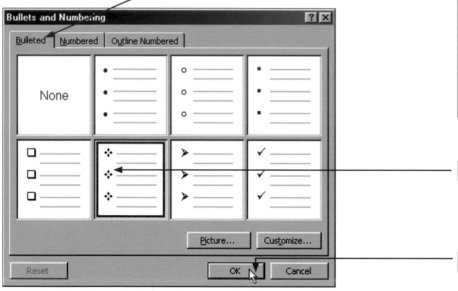

Bullets and Numbering

Bulleted | Numbered | Outline Numbered

None

Picture... Customize...

Reset   OK   Cancel

5 Click the **Bullet** type that you want.

6 Click **OK**.

A **Bullet** point will appear.

7 Type your text.

8 Press **Enter** to start the next **Bulleted** line.

How do I stop the **Bullet** *points?*

PE Kit
- ❖ Trainers
- ❖ Shorts
- ❖ T-Shirt
- ❖

- Go back to **2** and follow the instructions up to **5**.

- Click **None** for the **Bullet** type.

Going Shopping

SKILL: Using Bullet Points

You are going to make cheese on toast. You need a shopping list before you can start.

1 Open a **New** document.

2 Type the list below.

For the ingredients list, use **Bullets** of your choice. (See 37a)

```
                    Cheese on Toast

Ingredients
          ☐ Bread

          ☐ Margarine

          ☐ Cheese
```

3 Save.

You are also going to make pizza.

4 Open a **New** document.

5 Use **Bullets** and type a list of items that you might need to make a pizza. Use the **Bullets Icon** to add and remove your **Bullets**.

6 Save.

Bullets

Remember
*To remove or add a **Bullet**,*
your cursor needs to be
somewhere on that line.

1 Open a **New** document.

2 Type 'Reasons why I like my school'. Press **Enter**.

3 Click **Format**. ———————————————→

4 Click **Bullets and Numbering**. ————→

5 Click the **Numbered** tab.

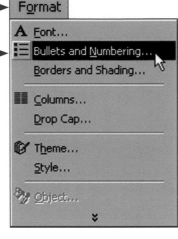

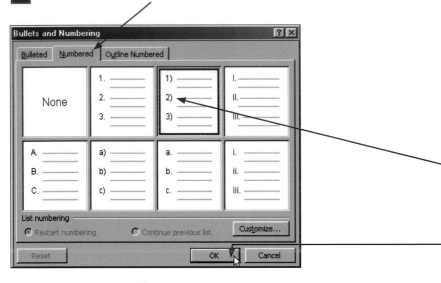

6 Click the **Numbering** style that you want.

7 Click **OK**.

A **Number** will appear.

8 Type your text.

9 Press **Enter** to start the next **Numbered** line.

How do I stop the **Numbering?**

● Go back to **3** and follow the instructions up to **5** .

● Click **None** for the **Numbering** type.

Make a Pizza

SKILL: Using Numbering

1 **Open** the document that you saved, listing the pizza ingredients. (See 37b)

2 Type instructions on how to 'Make a pizza'.

3 **Number** the instructions using the **Numbering** type of your choice. (See 38a)

4 Use the **Numbering** icon to add and remove your **Numbers**.

5 You may wish to change the **Font**, **Style**, **Size** or **Colour** of your text.

Numbering

6 **Save** and **Print**.

Placing Borders around the page

1 Open a **New** document.

2 Click **Format**.

3 Click **Borders and Shading**.

4 Click the **Page Border** tab.

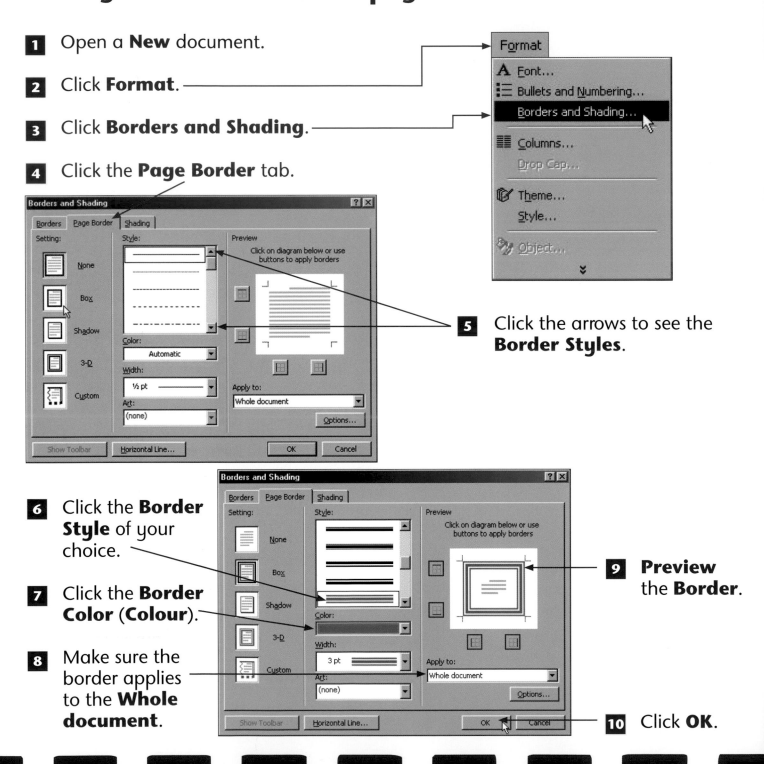

5 Click the arrows to see the **Border Styles**.

6 Click the **Border Style** of your choice.

7 Click the **Border Color (Colour)**.

8 Make sure the border applies to the **Whole document**.

9 **Preview** the **Border**.

10 Click **OK**.

1 Open the document that you saved for your circus poster.

2 Change the **Font Colour** of the poster.

3 Add a **Line Page Border** to the poster. (See 39a)

4 Check your work in **Print Preview**.

5 **Save** and **Print**.

Adding Art Page Borders

40a

SKILL

1 Open a **New** document.

2 Click **Format**.

3 Click **Borders and Shading**.

4 Click the **Page Border** tab.

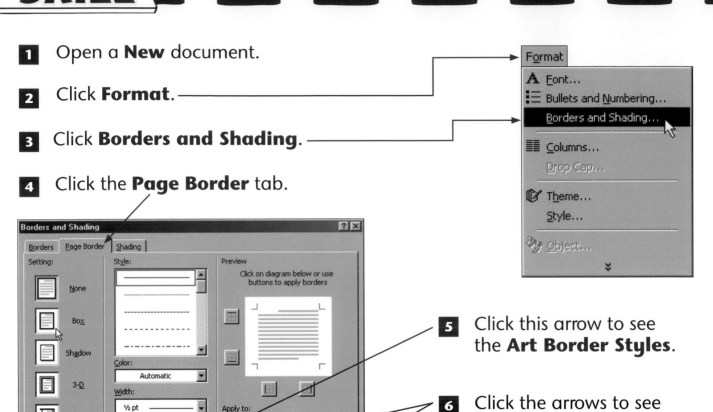

5 Click this arrow to see the **Art Border Styles**.

6 Click the arrows to see different **Border Styles**.

7 Click the **Border Style** of your choice.

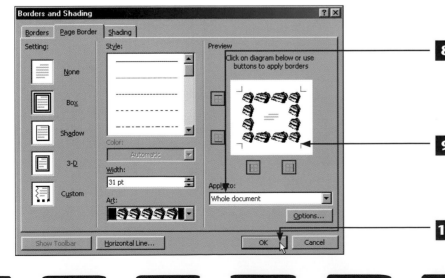

8 Make sure the **Border** applies to the **Whole document**.

9 **Preview** the **Border**.

10 Click **OK**.

Birthday Card

SKILL: Adding Art Page Borders

You are going to make a birthday card for one of your friends.

1 Open a **New** document.

2 Use **WordArt** to type 'Happy Birthday'. (See 33a)

3 Insert a **ClipArt**.

4 Insert an **Art Page Border**. (See 40a)

5 Check your work in **Print Preview**.

6 **Save** and **Print**.

Adding Borders

41a

SKILL

Placing borders around blocks of text

1 Open a **New** document.

2 Click **Format**.

3 Click **Borders and Shading**.

4 Click the **Borders** tab.

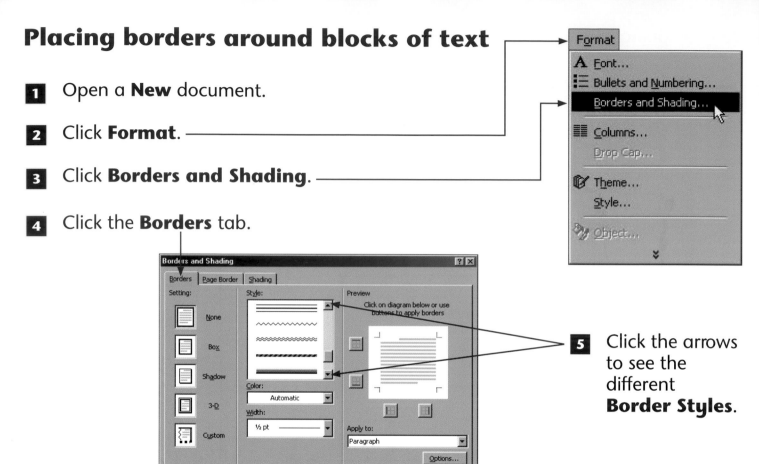

5 Click the arrows to see the different **Border Styles**.

6 Click a **Border Style**.

7 Click a **Border Colour**.

8 **Preview** the **Border**.

9 Click **OK**.

10 Type your text.

Zoo Signposts

SKILL: Adding Borders

The zoo needs the following signposts.

1 Open a **New** document.

> You will need a CD with animal **Pictures**.

● Lions	● Penguins
● Sea lions	● Tigers

2 Set-up a **Landscape** page.

3 Insert a **Border** of your choice. (See 41a)

4 Type the name of the first animal.

5 You may want to change the **Font**, **Style**, **Size** or **Colour** of the text.

6 Insert a matching animal **Picture** from the CD or ClipArt. (See 32a)

7 Check your work in **Print Preview**.

8 **Save** and **Print**.

10 Make signs for two more animals at the zoo. (Go back to **1**)

Using Shading

1 Open a **New** document.

2 Click **Format**.

3 Click **Borders and Shading**.

4 Click the **Shading** tab.

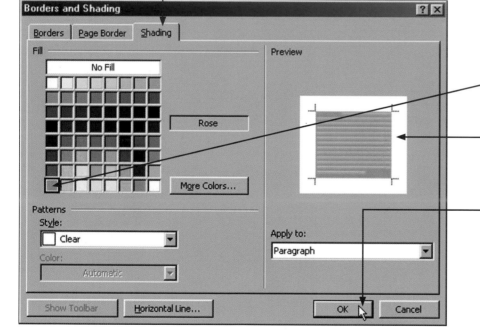

5 Click a **Fill** for the **Shading**.

6 **Preview** the **Shading**.

7 Click **OK**.

8 Type your text.

Now you can type with a background shading.

*You can add **Shading** to **Text Boxes** and **Borders**.*

9 After you have inserted a **Text Box** or **Border**, click on the shape and go to **2**.

WordWorks

Shading AutoShapes

SKILL: Using Shading

1 **Open** the document in which you saved your **AutoShapes**.

2 **Shade** each of the **AutoShapes**, using the **Fill** icon.

3 Click the arrow next to the **Fill** icon.

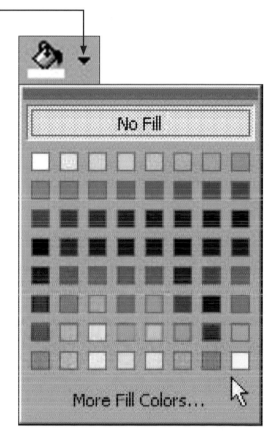

> When working with **AutoShapes**, you can only use the **Fill** icon to **Shade** the shapes.

No Fill

More Fill Colors...

4 Click on a **Fill Color (Colour)**.

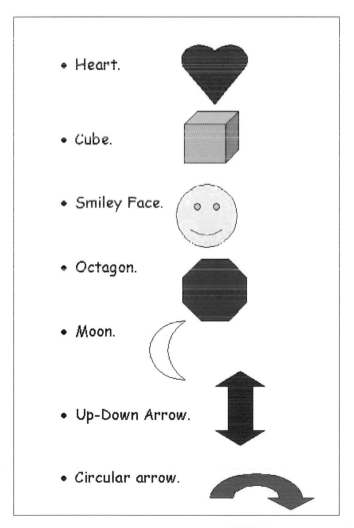

- Heart.
- Cube.
- Smiley Face.
- Octagon.
- Moon.
- Up-Down Arrow.
- Circular arrow.

5 **Save** and **Print**.

1 Open a **New** document.

2 Type your text.

3 Click the **I** in the line you want to start with a **Drop Cap**.

> I can enlarge the first letter of my story by using Drop Cap.

4 Click **Format**.

5 Click **Drop Cap**.

6 Click the **Position** of the **Drop Cap**.

Format

A Font...
≣ Bullets and Numbering...
    Borders and Shading...
▦ Columns...
    Drop Cap...
   Theme...
    Style...
   Object...
    ⌄

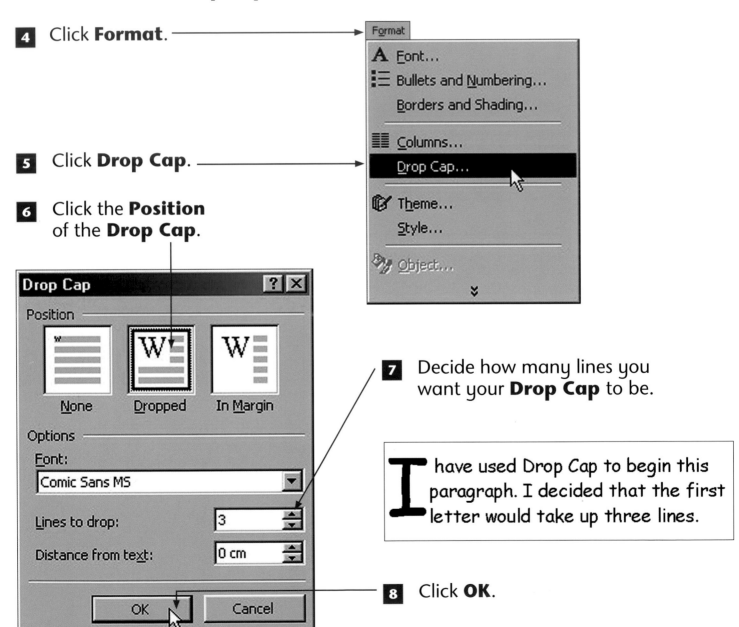

Drop Cap   ? X

Position

None   Dropped   In Margin

Options

Font:
Comic Sans MS

Lines to drop: 3

Distance from text: 0 cm

        OK   Cancel

7 Decide how many lines you want your **Drop Cap** to be.

> I have used Drop Cap to begin this paragraph. I decided that the first letter would take up three lines.

8 Click **OK**.

My Book

SKILL: Using Drop Cap

1 Open a **New** document.

2 Select **Font Size 20** and a **Font** of your choice.

3 Type the title of the book that you are reading now.

4 **Centre** the title. (See 14a)

TREASURE ISLAND

---

5 Press **Enter**.

6 Change the **Font Size** to **16**.

7 **Left Align** the text.

TREASURE ISLAND

PART ONE: The Old Buccaneer
1. The Old Sea Dog at the 'Admiral Benbow'

SQUIRE TRELAWNEY, Dr. Livesey, and the rest of these gentlemen having asked me to write down the whole particulars about Treasure Island, from the beginning to the end, keeping nothing back but the bearings of the island, and that only because there is still treasure not yet lifted, I take up my pen in the year of grace 17—, and go back to the time when my father kept the 'Admiral Benbow' inn, and the brown old seaman, with the sabre cut, first took up his lodging under our roof.

---

8 Use **Drop Cap** for the first letter of the opening paragraph. (See 43a)

9 **Save** and **Print**.

Using Columns

44a

SKILL

1 Open a **New** document.

2 Click **Format**.

3 Click **Columns**.

4 Click the number of **Columns** needed.

Format
A Font...
:≡ Bullets and Numbering...
   Borders and Shading...
▦ Columns...
   Drop Cap...
◱ Theme...
   Style...
⬧ Object...
   ⤵

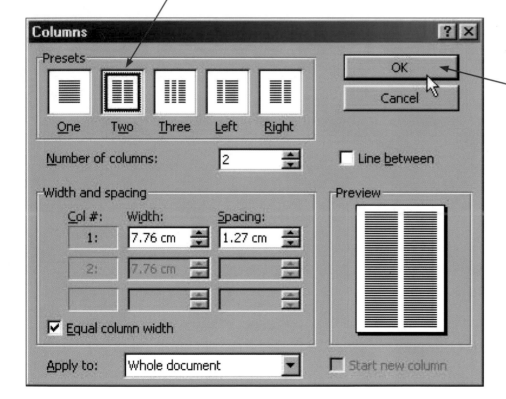

5 Click **OK**.

6 Type your text.

*You can put your text into **Columns** after you have typed.*

● **Highlight** the text you want to put into **Columns**.

● Go back to **2** and follow the instructions to **5**.

I can use columns to type in my text. This is my first column.

This is the second column.

WordWorks

School Newspaper

SKILL: Using Columns

APPLICATION

1. Open a **New** document.

2. Select **Font Size 28** and a **Font** of your choice.

3. Type the title of your newspaper article.

4. Press **Enter**.

5. Change the **Font Size** to **22**.

6. Type your newspaper story using two **Columns**. (See 44a)

7. Use **Drop Cap** for the first letter. (See 43a)

8. Check your work in **Print Preview**.

9. **Save** and **Print**.

School Sports Day

Yesterday was school sports day and it was a wonderful day. Raj Singh won the 100 metre sprint in a new school record time of 14.1 seconds. Jane Cotton won the long jump with a fantastic distance of 3.5 metres. In the teachers' egg and spoon race, Mrs Smith fell over before crossing the finishing line and Mr Ainsworth won. In the sack race, Narinda Patel stormed ahead to beat the rest of her class. The overall results were very close. The red team came fourth with 1100 points. The blue team came third with 1230 points. The yellow team were narrowly better than the blue team with 1250 points but victory was taken by the green team with 1300 points. Congratulations to all the competitors.

45a

SKILL

Change the case of existing text

1 Open a **New** document.

> I can change the case of my text.

2 Type your text.

3 **Highlight** your text by dragging the I over it, holding down the left mouse button.

4 Click **Format**. ————————————————

5 Click **Change Case**. ——————

6 Click a **Change Case** style.

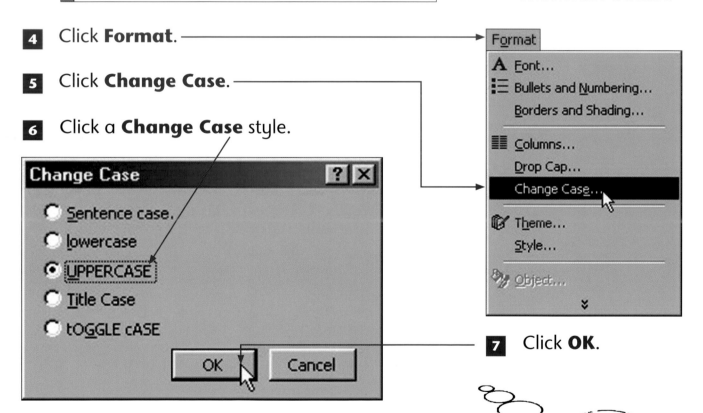

Change Case ?×

- ○ Sentence case.
- ○ lowercase
- ● UPPERCASE
- ○ Title Case
- ○ tOGGLE cASE

OK   Cancel

Format

- **A** Font...
- Bullets and Numbering...
- Borders and Shading...
- Columns...
- Drop Cap...
- Change Case...
- Theme...
- Style...
- Object...

7 Click **OK**.

Remember
*This does not work unless you **Highlight** the text first.*

> I CAN CHANGE THE CASE OF MY TEXT.

1 Open a **New** document.

2 Type the following sentences.

- THE SCHOOL FETE IS ON SUNDAY.

- the cat sat on the mat.

- beware of the dog!

- ON SATURDAYS I GO SWIMMING.

- please mind the step.

- I HAD A BAD COLD.

- happy birthday!

- warning!

- attention: the paint may be wet.

- I LIKE DOING MY WORK ON THE COMPUTER.

3 Change the case to suit each sentence, using **Change Case**. (See 45a)

4 **Save** and **Print**.

BEWARE OF THE DOG!

46a

SKILL

Justifying Text

1 Open a **New** document.

2 Find the **Justify** icon on your screen.

Justify

3 Click **Justify** icon. then type your text.

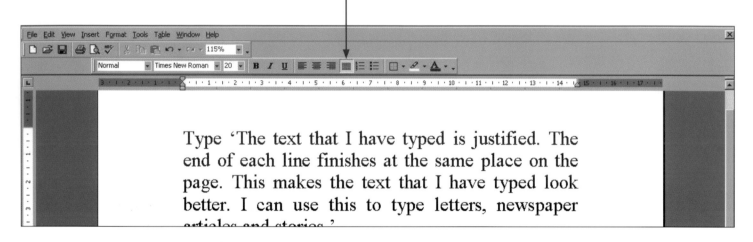

Type 'The text that I have typed is justified. The end of each line finishes at the same place on the page. This makes the text that I have typed look better. I can use this to type letters, newspaper articles and stories.'

What if I want to **Justify** *my text after I have typed it?*

● **Highlight** the words that you want to **Justify** by dragging the I over it, holding down the left mouse button.

● Click the **Justify** icon.

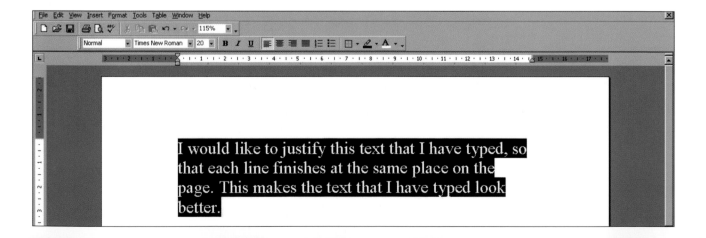

I would like to justify this text that I have typed, so that each line finishes at the same place on the page. This makes the text that I have typed look better.

SKILL: Justifying Text

1 **Open** the File that you saved your 'My Book' work in. (See 43b).

2 Change the **Font Colour** and **Font Style** of the title.

3 **Underline** the title. (See 13a)

4 Add another paragraph to your work.

5 **Justify** the text. (See 46a)

6 **Save** and **Print**.

TREASURE ISLAND

PART ONE: The Old Buccaneer
1. The Old Sea Dog at the 'Admiral Benbow'

SQUIRE TRELAWNEY, Dr. Livesey, and the rest of these gentlemen having asked me to write down the whole particulars about Treasure Island, from the beginning to the end, keeping nothing back but the bearings of the island, and that only because there is still treasure not yet lifted, I take up my pen in the year of grace 17—, and go back to the time when my father kept the 'Admiral Benbow' inn, and the brown old seaman, with the sabre cut, first took up his lodging under our roof.

I remember him as if it were yesterday, as he came plodding to the inn door, his sea-chest following behind him in a hand barrow; a tall, strong, heavy, nut-brown man; his tarry pigtail falling over the shoulders of his soiled blue coat; his hands ragged and scarred, with black, broken nails; and the sabre cut across one cheek, a dirty, livid white. I remember him looking round the cove and whistling to himself as he did so, and then breaking out in that old sea-song that he sang so often afterwards:

'Fifteen men on the dead man's chest –
Yo-ho-ho, and a bottle of rum!'

1 Open a **New** document.

2 Type the following text.

> I want to cheak the folowing for grammer. and spelling mistackes.

The words underlined with a red wavy line are spelling mistakes.
The words underlined with a green wavy line are grammatical mistakes.

3 Click **Tools**. ───────────────

4 Click **Spelling and Grammar**. ──────────

The **Spelling and Grammar** check will automatically go through all the words that it thinks are incorrect.

5 Click the correct spelling from the **Suggestions**.

Tools
- ✓ Spelling and Grammar... ⊤ ₹7
- Language ▶
- Protect Document...
- Envelopes and Labels...
- Letter Wizard...
- Macro ▶
- Customize...
- Options...
  ⌄

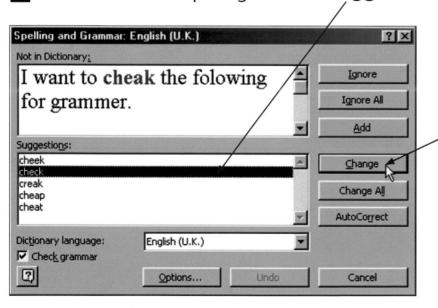

Spelling and Grammar: English (U.K.)   ? X

Not in Dictionary:

I want to **cheak** the folowing for grammer.

Ignore
Ignore All
Add
Change
Change All
AutoCorrect

Suggestions:
- cheek
- check
- creak
- cheap
- cheat

Dictionary language: English (U.K.)
☑ Check grammar

? | Options... | Undo | Cancel

6 Click **Change**.

7 Continue until you have checked all the text.

8 When the check is complete click **OK**.

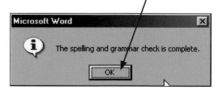

Microsoft Word   X
ⓘ The spelling and grammar check is complete.
OK

> *What if I know that it is the correct spelling and the spell checker suggests it is wrong?*

● Click **Ignore**.

SKILL: Checking Spelling and Grammar

1 Open a **New** document.

2 Type the following using a **Font** of your choice.

> • I were walking down the riad looking for a Post Office.
>
> • You was going to call me last night.
>
> • I were hiding from him in the bushes.
>
> • I likes fish anf chips.
>
> • I were going to the shop with me mum.

3 Check the **Spelling and Grammar**. (See 47a)

4 **Save** and **Print**.

48a

SKILL

1. Open a **New** document.

2. Type your text.

3. To find a different word for one you have typed, **Highlight** the word.

4. Click **Tools**.

5. Move to **Language**.

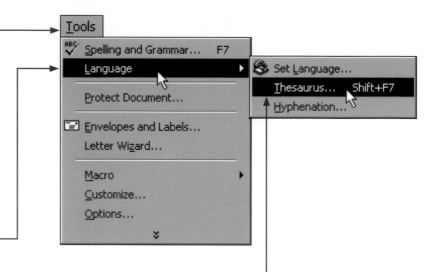

Tools
- Spelling and Grammar... F7
- Language ▶
  - Set Language...
  - Thesaurus... Shift+F7
  - Hyphenation...
- Protect Document...
- Envelopes and Labels...
- Letter Wizard...
- Macro ▶
- Customize...
- Options...

6. Click **Thesaurus**.

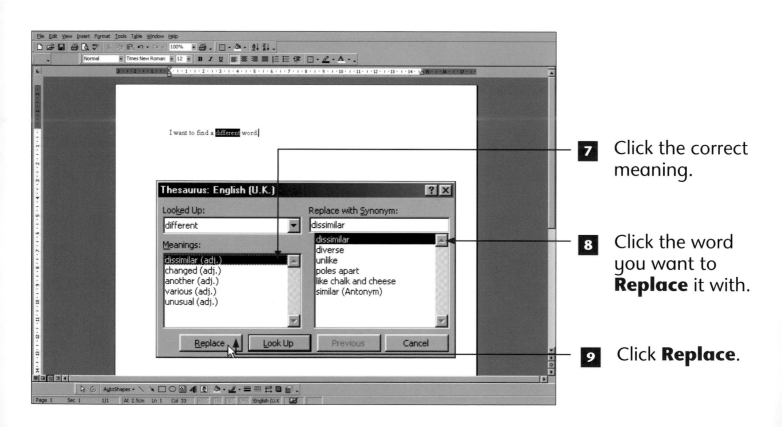

7. Click the correct meaning.

8. Click the word you want to **Replace** it with.

9. Click **Replace**.

1 Type each of the following words.

Able	Last
Bad	Made
Clear	End
Fear	Fable
Hobby	Turn

2 Use the **Thesaurus** to find an alternative word for each. (See 48a)

3 **Save** and **Print**.

Inserting Tables

1 Open a **New** document.

2 Click **Table**. ——————————→ Table

                                      Draw Table

3 Move to **Insert**. ——————————→ Insert ▸   ▸ Table...

                                    Delete ▸   Columns to the Left

                                    Select ▸   Columns to the Right

                                    Merge Cells   Rows Above

                                    Split Cells...   Rows Below

                                    Table AutoFormat...   Cells...

                                    Heading Rows Repeat

                                    Convert ▸

                                               4 Click **Table**.

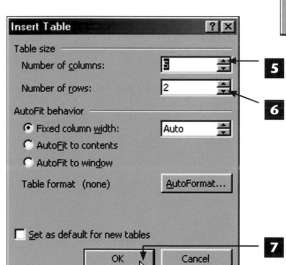

Insert Table ? ✕

Table size

Number of columns: 3 ↕ ——— **5** Click the arrows to set the **Number of columns**.

Number of rows: 2 ↕

AutoFit behavior   **6** Click the arrows to set the **Number of rows**.

◉ Fixed column width: Auto ↕

◯ AutoFit to contents

◯ AutoFit to window

Table format (none)   AutoFormat...

                                        How do I move to different boxes?

☐ Set as default for new tables

     OK   Cancel   **7** Click OK.

8 Type your text in the **Table**.

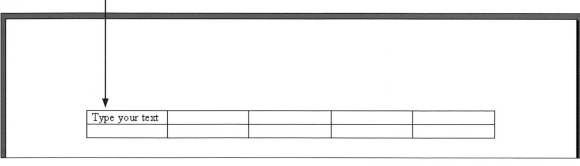

Type your text			

● Click the box where you want to type your text.

1 Open a **New** document.

2 Design a **Table** for the following information. (See 49a)

Circle: 1 Side

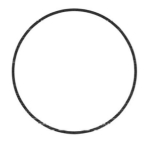

Triangle: 3 Sides

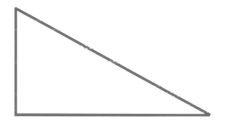

Square: 4 Sides

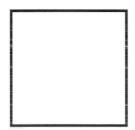

Hexagon: 6 Sides

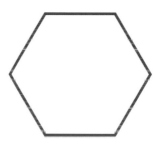

3 Enter the data in the **Table**.

4 **Save** and **Print**.

Editing Tables

Inserting Columns and Rows

1 Open a **New** document.

RedI	Blue
Green	Yellow

2 Create a **Table** like this with 2 columns and 2 rows. (See 49a)

3 Leave the cursor next to 'Red', in your **Table**.

4 Click **Table**.

5 Move to **Insert**.

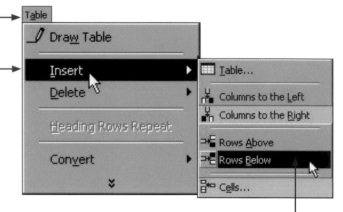

6 Click **Rows Below**.

Red	Blue
Green	Yellow

*If you leave the cursor next to 'Red' and **Insert – Rows Below**, this is what happens.*

Deleting Columns and Rows

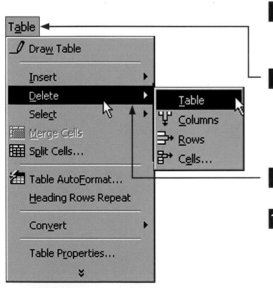

7 Leave your cursor in the **Table** on the **Row** or **Column** you want to **Delete**.

8 Click **Table**.

9 Move to **Delete**.

10 Click what you want to be **Deleted**.

Remember *If you want to **Delete** only one **Row** or one **Column**, your cursor has to be in that **Row** or **Column** before you click **Delete**.*

WordWorks © Folens (non-copiable)

Add Extra Rows and Data

SKILL: Editing Tables

50b

APPLICATION

1 **Open** the File that you saved your 'Shapes' table in. (See 49b)

Name of Shape	Number of Sides
Circle	1
Triangle	3
Square	4
Hexagon	6

To add three shapes to your table you will need to create three extra rows.

2 Use **Table – Insert – Rows**. (See 50a)

3 Type your additional information.

Name of Shape	Number of Sides
Circle	1
Triangle	3
Square	4
Pentagon	
Hexagon	6
	8
Decagon	

4 **Save** and **Print**.

Photocopying

Please note that pages from this book may **NOT** be photocopied.
The CLA licence does **NOT** apply to this book.

Editor: Emma Thomas
Layout artists: Patricia Hollingsworth and James Brown
Cover design: Patricia Harrison and Martin Cross
Illustrations: Jim Peacock
Photography: Corbis Stock Market, Paul Chauncey (page 79)

First published 2002 by Folens Limited.
Reprinted 2002, 2005.

Screenshots reprinted by permission from Microsoft Corporation.

Microsoft® and Word are either registered trademarks or trademarks of Microsoft Corporation in the United States and other countries.

Microsoft Word software is © 1983–2001 Microsoft Corporation. All rights reserved.

Every effort has been made to trace the copyright holders of material used in this publication. If any copyright holder has been overlooked, we should be pleased to make any necessary arrangements.

British Library Cataloguing in Publication Data. A catalogue record for this publication is available from the British Library.

ISBN 1 84303 132 9